HEALTH CARE IN TRANSITION

HEALTH CARE COSTS

POLICIES, ECONOMICS AND OUTCOMES

Health Care in Transition

Additional books in this series can be found on Nova's website under the Series tab.

Additional e-books in this series can be found on Nova's website under the e-book tab.

HEALTH CARE IN TRANSITION

HEALTH CARE COSTS

POLICIES, ECONOMICS AND OUTCOMES

BRANDON HILL
EDITOR

nova publishers
New York

Library of Congress Cataloging-in-Publication Data

ISBN: 978-1-63484-619-6

Published by Nova Science Publishers, Inc. † New York

CONTENTS

Preface **vii**

Chapter 1 Innovative Analytical Methods for Longitudinal Medical Cost Data: Translating Research to Inform Policy and Practice **1**
Lei Liu, Ya-Chen Tina Shih and Melford J. Henderson

Chapter 2 Application of da Vinci® Robot in General Surgery: A Cost Assessment **33**
Ioannis D. Gkegkes and Christos Iavazzo

Chapter 3 Cost Analysis of da Vinci® Robot Application in Gynaecological Operations **53**
Christos Iavazzo and Ioannis D. Gkegkes

Bibliography **75**

Index **121**

PREFACE

Rising health care cost is a major concern for health policy makers since the 1960s. Statistical analysis of medical cost data is becoming increasingly important with heightened interests in containing healthcare cost. In order to better understand the factors associated with the growth in medical expenditures, it is important to study the longitudinal history of medical care cost data.

Chapter 1 – The research provided in this book chapter is important for developing several new methods to enhance our understanding of how and why health care expenditures may change over time for an individual. It provides an excellent discussion of the contemporary issues in modeling medical costs, as well as new statistical models which are being developed for solving ongoing problems. The proposed research design is testing refinements/improvements to econometric models for analyzing longitudinal data on health care costs. The objective of this research is to develop and disseminate a number of models of medical costs in a longitudinal statistical framework that allows for the measurement of costs at regular intervals instead of only as a total (or cross-sectional cost). Additionally, this book chapter will emphasize practical application and policy of the methods and models presented. The specific aims are as follows: 1) to provide an overview of the currently available econometric and statistical models of medical costs to cross-sectional as well as longitudinal data; 2) to introduce the method of using more flexible functional forms of covariate specification (e.g., splines for non-linear temporal effects) in modeling longitudinal medical cost data.; 3) to describe an extension of the above flexible model to jointly analyze medical costs and multiple health outcomes (e.g., survival, or quality of life), and study the effect of risk factors on them simultaneously; 4) to discuss another extension that applies hierarchical models to address the clustering effect in modeling longitudinal medical cost data at different levels, e.g., health plans, families, and members; and 5) to present examples of practical application of the developed methods. The researchers will apply these new methods to three real-world databases: the Clinical Data Repository (CDR) at the University of Virginia Health System, the Medical Expenditure Panel Survey (MEPS), and the SEER-Medicare databases.

Chapter 2 – The utilization of robotic assisted surgical techniques represents a novelty in the field of general surgery. Moreover, the development of robotic technology facilitated the realization of complex operations both in hepatopancreatic and in colorectal surgery. However, the elevated costs of the robotic assisted surgery, in comparison to the other minimally invasive procedures, mainly the laparoscopic ones, make the application of robotics in general surgery expensive and not an everyday surgical technique. The present evidence reveals that robotic surgery, under specific conditions, has the potential to become cost-effective. Large number of cases, presence of industry competition and multidisciplinary team utilization are some of the factors that could make more reasonable and cost-effective the robotic assisted technique.

Chapter 3 – The application of robotics is an innovation in the field of gynecologic surgery. Specific characteristics of robotic assisted surgery, such as the 3-dimention view of the surgical field, the elimination of surgeon's natural tremor and the existence of wristed instruments, improve operator's dexterity and make easier every operation into the pelvis or retroperitoneally. On the other hand, the high cost of acquisition, maintenance and instrumentation, make the use of robotic systems an unaffordable luxury for countries of the developing world. Nevertheless, robotic surgery has the potential to become cost-effective in centers with many patients while industry competition could reduce the cost of the robotic instrumentation, making robotic technology more affordable and cost-effective.

In: Health Care Costs
Editor: Brandon Hill

ISBN: 978-1-63484-619-6

Chapter 1

INNOVATIVE ANALYTICAL METHODS FOR LONGITUDINAL MEDICAL COST DATA: TRANSLATING RESEARCH TO INFORM POLICY AND PRACTICE

***Lei Liu*[1], *Ya-Chen Tina Shih*[2] *and Melford J. Henderson*[3]**
[1]Northwestern University Feinberg School of Medicine, IL, US
[2]University of Texas MD Anderson Cancer Center, Houston, Texas, US
[3]Agency for Healthcare Research and Quality

ABSTRACT

Rising health care cost is a major concern for health policy makers since 1960s. Sisko et al. (2009) projected that health care costs per person will increase from $8,160 in 2009 to $13,100 in 2018, and that total health care costs will account for over 20% of the gross domestic product by 2018. Statistical analysis of medical cost data is becoming increasingly important with heightened interests in containing healthcare cost. In order to better understand the factors associated with the growth in medical expenditures, it is important to study the longitudinal history of medical care cost data. The research provided in this book chapter is important for developing several new methods to enhance our understanding of how and why health care expenditures may change over time for an individual. It provides an excellent discussion of the contemporary issues in modeling medical costs, as well as new statistical models which are being developed for solving ongoing problems. The proposed research design is testing refinements/improvements to econometric models for analyzing longitudinal data on health care costs. The objective of this research is to develop and disseminate a number of models of medical costs in a longitudinal statistical framework that allows for the measurement of costs at regular intervals instead of only as a total (or cross-sectional cost). Additionally, this book chapter will emphasize practical application and policy of the methods and models presented. The specific aims are as follows: 1) to provide an overview of the currently available econometric and statistical models of medical costs to cross-sectional as well as longitudinal data; 2) to introduce the method of using more flexible functional forms of covariate specification (e.g., splines for non-linear temporal effects) in modeling longitudinal medical cost data.; 3) to describe an extension of the above flexible model to jointly analyze medical costs and multiple health outcomes (e.g., survival, or quality of life), and study the effect of risk factors on them simultaneously; 4) to discuss another extension that applies hierarchical models to address the clustering effect in modeling longitudinal medical cost data at different levels, e.g., health plans, families, and members; and 5) to present examples of practical application of the developed methods. The researchers will apply these new methods to three real-world databases: the Clinical Data Repository (CDR) at the University of Virginia Health System, the Medical Expenditure Panel Survey (MEPS), and the SEER-Medicare databases.

Introduction and Purpose

Policy makers' interest in health care cost containment strategies has made statistical analysis of medical cost data increasingly important. To better understand the factors associated with the growth in medical costs, it is important to study the history of longitudinal medical data. Medical cost data are routinely collected in billing records of hospitals and claims of health insurance plans (e.g., Medicare, Medicaid, or commercial insurance). The wide availability of such data has motivated the development and application of state-of-the-art statistical and econometric methods. With technological advances in automated data collection and management techniques, medical costs are now often gathered at regular time intervals (e.g., monthly or even daily), creating a longitudinal data pattern. Most of the literature to date has focused on modeling total costs, or annual costs; little work has examined statistical models for costs disaggregated to finer time intervals or models that account for the longitudinal pattern of medical costs data.

The analysis of longitudinal cost data is central to the understanding of the dynamics of medical costs and different paths of cost trajectories over time. Ignoring the medical cost history by fitting the model with cross-sectional data can be inefficient and sometimes inaccurate as important information, such as the time pattern of critical medical events, may be lost in the cross-sectional models. Several researchers have attested the importance of longitudinal assessment of medical cost data. Heitjan et al. (2004) emphasized that such analysis provides a more detailed understanding of the processes of cost accrual and the reasons for cost differences between interventions. Yabroff et al. (2009) noted that longitudinal estimates of medical costs after diagnosis could assist policy makers in determining resource allocation and treatment coverage for a specific disease. In many circumstances the timing and duration of the treatment (and the costs thus incurred) are key concerns for medical practitioners and researchers. Describing the temporal trend of medical costs is an important goal because knowing that for specific diagnoses or for a select subgroup of patients the majority of medical costs will be incurred in the initial six months after diagnosis, as opposed to being uniformly spread out over years or concentrated during the last few weeks of treatment, has *implications* for when and how frequently one might want to initiate utilization review measures or launch disease management programs. For example, Liu (2009) documented a pattern of increasing utilization of medical services one year after the initial diagnosis or treatment of heart failure, noting that knowledge of this pattern can assist clinicians, patients, and their families in making special arrangements for patients at that disease stage.

Longitudinal Assessment of Cost in Health Care Interventions

A. Analytical Issues Commonly Encountered in the Analysis of Longitudinal Medical Cost Data

A1. Empirical Challenges in Analyzing Medical Costs Data

Analyses of medical costs data are complicated by several characteristics of such data (Lipscomb et al. 2009). First, a large portion of medical costs may be zero (i.e., mass zero) because certain medical care services (e.g., hospitalization) are utilized by a small percentage of the population, leaving medical cost associated with these services to be zero for a large number of observations (i.e., the non-users). Second, medical cost data tend to be highly skewed to the right because a small percentage of the population consumed a disproportionally large share of healthcare expenditures. For example, analysis using the 2009 Medical Expenditure Panel Survey showed that over 20% of all health care spending in 2009 was consumed by 1% of the population. Lastly, medical cost data are often heteroscedastic because heterogeneity across individuals may cause the variance of costs to differ across different subgroups. For example, the variance of medical cost for healthy individuals is likely much smaller than that for those in poor health because a wide range of health seeking behavior (and thus medical costs) is more likely to be observed among individuals in poor health.

A2. Longitudinal Medical Cost Data

A.2.1. Why Are the Data Important?

As mentioned previously, longitudinal medical cost data offers important information on the process of cost accrual and the understanding of such process can assist policy makers in resource allocation and coverage decisions (Heitjan et al. 2004; Yabroff et al. 2009). However, there are additional analytical issues to be considered when analyzing longitudinal medical cost data. First, medical costs accumulated within different time intervals are correlated for the same subjects. For example, a patient with higher medical care costs in the past is more likely to have higher costs in the future. Second, it is possible that a patient with a higher probability of zero cost (i.e., with no utilization of medical treatment) is healthier and would thus incur lower costs if treated. That is, "how often the patient sees doctors" and "how much it costs" could be correlated. All these issues suggest that simple models are not sufficient to analyze longitudinal medical cost data appropriately.

Longitudinal analysis of medical costs plays an important role in understanding the impact of health policy changes on medical expenditures. An example can be found in the change of reimbursement policy regarding erythropoietin (EPO) by the Centers for Medicare and Medicaid Services (CMS). In June 1989, the FDA approved EPO for the treatment of anemia in patients undergoing dialysis. EPO quickly became the single largest expenditure for drugs covered by Medicare. Since 1989 the CMS has changed the reimbursement policy six times in response to the FDA's modifications of the target hematocrit range, resulting in dramatic variations of Medicare expenditures on EPO over time. Cotter et al. (2006) studied how the Medicare expenditures on EPO fluctuated following changes in the reimbursement policy and found that Medicare expenditures on EPO grew from $246 million in 1991 to $735 million in 1997, and then leveled off several months after the CMS enacted a stricter rule on the target hematocrit level. This study exemplifies how analysis of longitudinal medical costs can provide important insight on how the change in health policy affects medical spending patterns at individual level.

In addition to the policy significance, information on longitudinal medical costs is also important for patients and their families. By projecting financial burden of an illness, such information can help patients and their family members plan ahead, which reduces some of the fear of unknown financial burdens and may help to alleviate related anxiety, depression and worsening health.

A.2.2. Data Availability

A major source of longitudinal medical cost data is administrative database. In the United States, such data can be obtained from public and private insurance or healthcare system. Commonly used claims data from public insurance include: Medicare claims, Medicaid claims, and SEER-Medicare database which linked Medicare claims to cancer registry SEER. Private insurance claims data, such as MarketScan and LifeLink data, are often proprietary and can be licensed from private vendors. Examples of administrative data from healthcare systems are the Clinical Data Repository at the University of Virginia Health System, or data from Kaiser. A detailed overview of large databases, along with their strengths and limitations, can be found in Jagsi et al. (2014). Longitudinal medical cost data can also be obtained from longitudinal surveys, such as the Medical Expenditure Panel Survey.

B. Overview of Econometric Methods to Analyze Medical Costs in Cross-Sectional Data

Modeling medical costs is an important topic in the health economics literature. To address analytical issues commonly encountered in the analysis medical cost data, a number of statistical and econometric models have been proposed for cross-sectional medical cost data.

Characteristics of medical costs data, such as mass zero, a highly skewed distribution, and heteroscedasticity, often lead to semi-continuous data structure. Recognizing the need to account for the semi-continuous nature of medical cost data began with the development of the "two-part" model (2PM; Cragg 1971; Manning et al. 1981). Manning et al. (1981) applied the 2PM to cross-sectional medical cost data. Denote the cost of a given subject by Y. A 2PM for the probability distribution of Y consists of (i) modeling the probability that $Y > 0$ using a logistic or probit model ("Part I"); and, (ii) separately modeling the probability distribution of $Y|Y > 0$ ("Part II"). That is, the model separates zero cost and positive cost. Let U_i denote whether the cost for person i is positive, i.e.,

$$U_i = \begin{cases} 1, \text{if } Y_i > 0 \\ 0, \text{otherwise} \end{cases}$$

Define $\pi_i = P(U_i = 1)$. The two-part model can be written as follows:

$$\text{logit}\ (\pi_i) = X_i^T \alpha \qquad \text{(B1-A)}$$

$$\log Y_i |\ (Y_i > 0) = X_i^T \beta + \varepsilon_i \qquad \text{(B1-B)}$$

where X_i is the covariate vector, α and β are regression coefficients, T is the matrix transpose operator, and ε_i is the error term with zero mean. In the two-part model, model (B1-A) divides the population into non-users and users by a logit function, whereas model (B1-B) uses the log transformation of the medical costs as the response and applies a classical linear regression method.

A number of methods were developed to deal with the common presence of skewness and heteroscedasticity in medical cost data. A convenient and probably most common method is to assume that [log(Y) | $Y > 0$] follows a linear regression model with a normal error term (Manning et al. 1981; Diehr et al. 1999). However, since decision makers are not interested in dollars on the log scale *per se*, retransformation methods, such as the smearing technique proposed by Duan (1983), was proposed to transform the log cost back to its original scale (i.e., in dollars). Researchers have also found that when there is heteroscedasticity, the estimated regression coefficients from the OLS model with log(cost) as the dependent variable are biased (Manning 1998, Mullahy 1998, Manning and Mullahy 2001), which motivated the next wave of methodological development in health econometrics.

By the late 1990s, the method commonly used to analyze medical cost data was the generalized linear model (GLM) with costs in the original scale to simultaneously model the skewed and heteroscedastic medical cost data (Manning 1998; Mullahy 1998; Blough, Madden, and Hornbrook 1999; Manning and Mullahy 2001; Buntin and Zaslavsky 2004; Manning, Basu, and Mullahy 2005).

These methods employed the link and variance structure by fixed functions, such as log link with gamma error distribution, and implemented the estimation via quasi-likelihood methods (McCullagh and Nelder 1989). The superior performance of the GLM models over linear models with log transformed costs was supported in numerous simulation studies (Manning and Mullahy 2001; Buntin and Zaslavsky 2004; Manning, Basu, and Mullahy 2005).

More recently, a more general form of GLM was proposed by Basu and Rathouz (2005). This method, known as the extended estimating equations (EEE) method, specifies the mean model (for non-zero cost) as an extension of the Box-Cox link (EQ (B2-A)). Regression parameters β and the link parameters λ are estimated via a quasi-likelihood function.

$$g(\mu_i) = X_i^T\beta = \begin{cases} (\mu_i^\lambda - 1)/\lambda \text{ if } \lambda \neq 0 \\ \log(\mu_i) \text{ if } \lambda = 0 \end{cases} \tag{B2-A}$$

The variance function can be specified as cither the power variance family with

$$\text{Var}(Y_i) = \theta_1\mu_i^{\theta_2} \tag{B2-B}$$

or the quadratic variance family with

$$\text{Var}(Y_i) = \theta_1\mu_i + \theta_2\mu_i^2 \tag{B2-C}$$

where θ_1 and θ_2 are parameters. Many earlier versions of econometric model for medical cost analysis were nested under the EEE model.

C. Recent Methodological Advances in Analyzing Longitudinal Medical Cost Data

Compared to the rich literature available on the analysis of cross-sectional medical cost data, the sophistication of statistical /econometric theories and computational complexity have limited the application of the methods developed for modeling cross-sectional medical cost data directly to the analysis longitudinal medical cost data, as evident by the paucity of related publications in the literature. Section C introduces recently developed innovative statistical and econometric methods for longitudinal medical cost data.

C1. Random Effects Multi-Part Models for Longitudinal Medical Cost Data

C.1.1. Random Effects Two-Part Model for Correlated Medical Costs

When applying the two-part model to longitudinal medical cost data, the frequency and cost of medical services can be correlated over time since healthier patients are less likely to seek medical care, and when seeking medical care they tend to incur lower costs. To address this analytical issue, Olsen and Schafer (2001), and Tooze, Grunwald and Jones (2002) extended the two-part model to account for both the within- and cross-part correlations through the introduction of random effects. Let Y_{ij} denote the actual monthly medical cost for the j-th month of subject i, and U_{ij} denote the indicator of non-zero cost. Conditional on covariates and random effects, the probability of positive cost $\pi_{ij} = P(U_{ij} = 1)$ is as follows:

$$\text{logit}\, \pi_{ij} = X_{ij}^T \alpha + a_i \tag{C1-A}$$

where X_{ij} is the covariate vector, α is the regression coefficient, and a_i is the random effect to account for the correlation in the longitudinal binary outcome of cost being positive within the same subject. Hereafter, for simplicity of notation, we include only the random intercept in the models we discuss. Other random effects, e.g., random slope, can be easily added into the model.

Assume that the non-zero monthly medical costs can be transformed (e.g., log transformation) to have a normal distribution, the second part can then be written as follows:

$$\log Y_{ij} \mid (Y_{ij} > 0) = X_{ij}^T \beta + c_i + \varepsilon_{ij} \tag{C1-B}$$

where c_i is the random effect to account for the correlation in the level of monthly positive cost within the same subject. The error term $\varepsilon_{ij} \sim N(0, \sigma_\varepsilon^2)$ is independent of random effects a_i and c_i.

Denote $r_i = \begin{pmatrix} a_i \\ c_i \end{pmatrix} \sim N(0, \Sigma)$, where $\Sigma = \begin{pmatrix} \sigma_a^2 & \sigma_{ac} \\ \sigma_{ac} & \sigma_c^2 \end{pmatrix}$ is the positive definite covariance matrix for random effects. The random effects a_i and c_i, respectively, account for the variation within the same subject in Parts I and II. The correlation between a_i and c_i, or the off-diagonal element σ_{ac}, captures the cross-part correlation between the odds of non-zero cost and the level of positive cost within the same subject. That is, $\sigma_{ac} > 0$ if patients who more frequently utilize medical care services also tend to incur higher monthly medical costs when treated. If Σ is diagonal ($\sigma_{ac} = 0$), then the two outcomes are independent of each other. A reduced model with two independent equations can be fitted as a naive method.

Liu, Strawderman, Cowen, and Shih (2010) further extended the above model, using the three-parameter (location, shape and scale) g-Gamma distribution to model the correlated medical cost data in a longitudinal setting. This model first specifies whether the correlated medical costs are positive:

$$\text{logit } \pi_{ij} = X_{ij}^T \alpha + a_i . \tag{C2-A}$$

Then the model lets the location parameter in the g-Gamma distribution depend on both fixed effects β and random effects c_i, as specified below:

$$\mu_{ij} = X_{ij}^T \beta + c_i . \tag{C2-B}$$

This model assumes random effects $r_i = \begin{pmatrix} a_i \\ c_i \end{pmatrix} \sim N(0, \Sigma)$, and as in Manning, Basu and Mullahy (2005), it also accounts for heteroscedasticity in medical costs by assuming the scale parameter σ depends on risk factors, i.e.,

$$\sigma^2 = \exp(X_{ij}^T \delta). \tag{C2-C}$$

The above flexible random effects two-part model has the advantage of being very comprehensive and is able to include many other models as special cases, e.g., log-normal, gamma, and Weibull.

It should be noted that other flexible distributions can be used to capture the characteristics of highly skewed and heteroscedastic data. For example, Liu et al. (2015) reviewed and considered three random effects two-part models in describing longitudinal semi-continuous data, assuming that the positive values follow (1) generalized gamma distribution, (2) log-skew-normal distribution, and (3) normal distribution after the Box-Cox transformation. Heteroscedasticity is incorporated into all three models, and each can be implemented in SAS Proc NLMIXED in a convenient way, making them accessible to general statistical practitioners. The relative performance can be compared using likelihood ratio tests for model selection and non-nested hypotheses.

C.1.2. Random Effects Four-Part Model for Longitudinal Medical Costs

Liu et al. (2008) extended the four-part model (Duan et al. 1983) to longitudinal medical cost setting. Specifically, define by V_{ij} the indicator of any inpatient cost for month j, the four part model is:

$$\text{logit}\, P(U_{ij} = 1) = X_{ij}^T \alpha + a_i, \quad \text{(C3-A)}$$

$$\text{logit}\, P(V_{ij} = 1) = X_{ij}^T \gamma + b_i, \quad \text{(C3-B)}$$

$$\log Y_{ij} \,|(U_{ij} = 1 \,\&\, V_{ij} = 0) = X_{ij}^T \beta + c_i + \varepsilon_{ij}, \quad \text{(C3-C)}$$

$$\log Y_{ij} \,|(V_{ij} = 1) = X_{ij}^T \eta + d_i + e_{ij}, \quad \text{(C3-D)}$$

where the first and second outcomes are the probability of any cost and inpatient costs, respectively, and the third and fourth outcomes are the amount of outpatient and inpatient costs, respectively.

This random-effect four-part model posits that $r_i = (a_i, b_i, c_i, d_i)^T \sim N(0, \Sigma)$, where Σ is the positive definite covariance matrix for random effects. Conditional on random effects r_i, the model assumes that the four outcomes are independent. The joint distribution defines the correlation ("cross-part correlation") among repeated measures. For example, patients with a greater probability of positive monthly costs are in poorer health, therefore they are more likely to be hospitalized and incur inpatient costs. Also, patients with higher outpatient monthly costs are expected to have higher inpatient monthly costs.

C.2. Semiparametric Models for Nonlinear Covariate Effects

In the analysis of longitudinal medical cost data, there often exists a temporal trend. Such a temporal trend, however, often presents a non-linear pattern. For example, many researchers have observed a "bathtub" or a U-shaped pattern (Lin et al. 1997; Bang and Tsiatis 2000; Brown et al. 2002; Etzioni et al. 2002; Liu, Wolfe, and Kalbfleisch 2007; Yabroff et al. 2009) for medical costs. This pattern is characterized by three phases: high initial costs for diagnosis and active treatment immediately after diagnosis, followed by a period of relatively flat medical costs when patients are in stable medical condition, and finally a sharp increase in medical costs during the time period prior to death because of intensive end-of-life medical care. In addition, other covariates, e.g., age, could also affect medical cost in a non-linear pattern (Chen et al. 2013, 2015B, Sun 2015). These non-linear patterns cannot be sufficiently addressed with simple methods such as adding quadratic and higher-order functional terms in the regression models (Liu, Huang and O'Quigley 2008). More sophisticated statistical methods, e.g., splines, are necessary to accurately capture such non-linear patterns, as failure to account for the non-linear pattern could lead to incorrect assessments of relationships and/or significance as well as impaired predictions.

C.2.1. Overview of Models with Non-Linear Covariate Effect for Cross-Sectional Data

Semiparametric regression methods have been used to capture nonlinear covariate effects. Using Part II of a two-part model as an example, a semiparametric model can be incorporated into an OLS model as follows:

$$\log Y_i | (Y_i > 0) = f(X_{1i}) + X_{2i}^T \beta + \varepsilon_i \tag{C4}$$

In this model, X_{1i} is a continuous variable (e.g., age) that has an unknown non-linear covariate effect (denoted by an unknown smooth function $f(\cdot)$) on the log costs, while X_{2i} contains all other variables that are linearly related to the log costs with a slope vector β. The error term ε_i is assumed to follow a normal distribution with mean 0 and variance σ_ε^2.

This model specification implies that different covariates have different functional relations with the medical costs. Some continuous covariates (e.g., age) could have non-linear relations with the log costs, whose functional form is of interest. Other covariates (continuous or discrete) have linear relations with the log costs. The main advantages of this semiparametric model over the polynomial function approach are flexibility and stability. If non-linear patterns and non-constant variance (heteroscedasticity) are present in the data, a higher-degree polynomial function is required to reasonably go through the data. However, the higher-degree fit has wiggles that are not representative of any features in the data. In a semiparametric model, the shape of the functional relationship is determined by the data. We assume $f(\cdot)$ to be a smoothing function, the estimation of which could be obtained by either kernels or splines (Ruppert et al., 2003).

The above model assumes that medical costs follow the lognormal distribution. In reality, the lognormal distribution may not be sufficient. Other more general distributions, e.g., generalized Gamma, could be used to give more robust estimates. As an alternative, GLMs that specify only the mean and variance, rather than the density function, could be more suitable for skewed and heteroscedastic medical cost data. For example, Chen et al. (2013A) extended the EEE method (Basu and Rathouz (2005) as follows:

$$\log(\mu_i) = f(X_{1i}) + X_{2i}^T\beta, \quad \text{(C5-A)}$$

$$\text{Var}(Y_i) = \sigma^2(\mu_i), \quad \text{(C5-B)}$$

where both $f(\cdot)$ and $\sigma^2(\cdot)$ are unknown smooth functions; X_{1i} and X_{2i} are defined similarly to those in model (C4). This model is especially appealing when there exists different functional forms for different covariates on the impact of the mean medical cost, whereas in the EEE models all covariates are restricted to having the same functional relation with the outcome. Also, the variance function is an unspecified smooth function, which is more flexible than the specified parametric function in the EEE.

C.2.2. Random Effects Approach for Longitudinal Data

To capture the non-linear covariate effect on longitudinal medical costs, Sun et al. (2015) proposed the following model:

$$\log Y_{ij} \mid Y_{ij} > 0 = f(X_{1ij}) + X_{2ij}^T \beta + c_i + \varepsilon_{ij}, \quad \text{(C6)}$$

where X_{1ij} is a vector of continuous variables (e.g., age) whose functional form $f(\cdot)$ could be non-linear on log positive cost; X_{2ij} contains all the other variables that are linearly related to the log positive cost; c_i is the random effect to capture the correlation among repeated measures of costs within the same subject; and ε_{ij} is the error term. The unknown function $f(\cdot)$ is estimated by the kernel method.

C.2.3. Marginal Approach for Longitudinal Data

Chen et al. (2015B) extended model (C5) to the longitudinal medical cost setting as follows:

$$\log(\mu_{ij}) = f(X_{1ij}) + X_{2ij}^T \beta \quad \text{(C7-A)}$$

$$\text{Var}(Y_{ij}) = \sigma^2(\mu_{ij}) \quad \text{(C7-B)}$$

$$\text{cov}(Y_{ij}, Y_{ik}) = \phi(\mu_{ij}, \mu_{ik}) \quad \text{(C7-C)}$$

An unspecified function $\phi(\cdot)$ is included in Eqn. (C7-C) for the covariance structure among the repeated measures of medical costs within the same subject. This model adopts a GEE-like approach, assuming a "working correlation" matrix in (C7-C) when estimating both linear and non-linear parameters in Eqns. (C7-A) and (C7-B).

When there exist a large number of continuous covariates which might have nonlinear relationship with the outcome, it is computationally challenging to model each covariate by a separate nonlinear function. In this case, one can consider the use of a single index model to reduce the dimension of covariates, by assuming that the parametric part ($X_{ij}^T \alpha$, known as the scalar "index") has a nonlinear relation with medical cost, i.e.,

$$\log \mu_{ij} = f(X_{ij}^T \alpha) + Z_{ij}^T \beta + c_i, \quad \text{(C8)}$$

where $X_{ij} = (X_{ij1}, X_{ij2}, \ldots)^T$ is the vector of all continuous covariates which may affect the outcome in an unspecified manner, and Z_{ij} is vector for covariate with a linear relationship. The advantage of the single index model is that it only has a single nonparametric function; thus, simplifying the computation and interpretation. Chen et al. (2015A) used such a single index model to study health costs for alcohol-dependent individuals in a naltrexone clinical trial.

C.2.4. Semiparametric Model in Random Effects 2PM

In the context of two-part model where Part I and Part II are considered simultaneously, smooth functions can be added in both parts to flexibly describe the non-linear covariate effect. Chen et al. (2013B) presented a semiparametric model in random effects 2PM, i.e.,

$$\text{logit } \pi_{ij} = g(X_{1ij}) + X_{2ij}^T \alpha + a_i \qquad \text{(C9-A)}$$

$$\log Y_{ij} \mid (Y_{ij} > 0) = f(X_{1ij}) + X_{2ij}^T \beta + c_i + \varepsilon_{ij} \qquad \text{(C9-B)}$$

where $f(\cdot)$ and $g(\cdot)$ are unknown non-linear functions. Here the model assumes X_{1ij} is non-linear in both parts for ease of notation, however, a covariate could have a linear effect in Part I, but a non-linear effect in Part II, or vice versa. Similar to the previous models, this model also assumes $r_i = \begin{pmatrix} a_i \\ c_i \end{pmatrix} \sim N(0, \boldsymbol{\Sigma})$, where $\boldsymbol{\Sigma} = \begin{pmatrix} \sigma_a^2 & \sigma_{ac} \\ \sigma_{ac} & \sigma_c^2 \end{pmatrix}$ is the positive definite covariance matrix for the random effects. The correlation between a_i and c_i, or the off-diagonal element σ_{ac}, describes the cross-part correlation between the odds of positive cost and the level of positive cost within the same subject.

D. Review of Methods of Joint Modeling of Costs and Health Outcomes

In addition to medical costs, researchers are often also interested in exploring the relationship between medical costs and health outcomes. Medical costs can be closely related to mortality or other health outcomes because a patient with a poor health tends to accumulate high medical costs, report a lower quality of life, and have a higher risk of death. Furthermore, medical costs increase dramatically with proximity to death (Stearns and Norton 2004). However, the relation between medical costs and mortality is not always obvious and could present a somewhat counterintuitive pattern: higher costs for patients with moderate but chronic disease vs. lower costs for patients with more severe disease that leads to poor survival. Examples of such pattern can be found in several studies. Lin et al. (1997) showed that for epithelial ovarian cancer, long-term costs are highest for those diagnosed with mild localized cancer (lower stage) and lowest for those with the most severe distant metastasis (higher stage). Bang and Tsiatis (2002) noticed that the total medical costs for colorectal cancer patients diagnosed at stage IV were lower than for those diagnosed at stage II. Lubitz et al. (2003) showed that the expected cumulative health expenditures for healthier elderly persons, despite their greater longevity, were similar to those for less healthy persons. All these studies suggest that better health does not necessarily lead to lower lifetime medical costs. These puzzling patterns have motivated statisticians to develop joint models for longitudinal medical costs and mortality to capture the complex relationship between costs and health outcomes.

D.1. Joint Modeling Longitudinal Medical Costs and Mortality

Liu, Wolfe and Kalbfleisch (2007) first considered a joint model of longitudinal medical costs and mortality to analyze monthly outpatient erythropoietin costs extracted from Medicare outpatient dialysis claims. The model, specified in EQ(D1) below, uses random effects to capture the correlation among medical costs collected over different time intervals, and then incorporated the random effects in the Cox proportional hazards model for mortality:

$$\log\,(Y_{ij}+1) \;=\; X_{ij}^T\,\beta + a_i + \varepsilon_{ij} \qquad \text{(D1-A)}$$

$$\lambda_i(t) \;=\; \lambda_0(t)\exp(X_i^T\delta + \gamma a_i) \qquad \text{(D1-B)}$$

where $\lambda_i(t)$ is the death hazard for subject i, $\lambda_0(t)$ is the baseline hazard, and γ is the coefficient for random effects a_i. The inclusion of random effects a_i in the hazard model introduces a mechanism to account for the correlation between longitudinal medical costs and survival, after adjusting for the observed risk factors. A positive γ would suggest that medical costs and mortality are positively correlated; that is, patients with poorer health tend to spend more on monthly medical costs, and they are also at a higher risk of death.

D.2. Joint Modeling Longitudinal Semi-Continuous Medical Costs and Survival

Of note, model (D1-A) takes log transformation on $(Y+1)$ to address the zero mass in medical costs. The above model was further extended to a two-part random effects model by Liu (2009) to address the "semi-continuous" issue, adding the random effects from the two-part model to the hazard model. This modified joint model is shown below:

$$\text{logit}\;\pi_{ij} \;=\; X_{ij}^T\,\alpha + a_i \qquad \text{(D2-A)}$$

$$\log\,Y_{ij}\,|\,(Y_{ij}>0) \;=\; X_{ij}^T\,\beta + c_i + \varepsilon_{ij} \qquad \text{(D2-B)}$$

$$\lambda_i(t) = \lambda_0(t)\exp(X_i^T\delta + \gamma_1 a_i + \gamma_2 c_i) \quad \text{(D2-C)}$$

where γ_1 and γ_2 are coefficients for random effects a_i (from Part I) and c_i (from Part II), respectively. An assumption in this model is that the mortality rate is correlated with both the likelihood of utilizing medical care services and the amount of medical costs. This is because a sicker patient is likely to have a higher risk of death and a higher likelihood of seeking medical treatment as well as receiving more intensive care when treated, resulting in higher monthly medical costs.

D.3. Analysis of Longitudinal Medical Cost Data in the Presence of Informative Observational Times and a Dependent Terminal Event

In some circumstances, medical costs in longitudinal data can serve as a marker of recurrent events. For example, the medical costs for each hospital visit may operate as a marker of the recurrent events of the hospital visit: they are correlated in that higher costs are associated with a higher rate of hospital admission. Such data are sometimes called “recurrent marker” data. Liu, Huang, and O'Quigley (2008) considers medical costs incurred during each hospital visit to be repeated measures recorded at informative observational times, similar to Lin and Ying (2001), Lin et al. (2004), and Sun et al. (2005). They presented a joint model of recurrent hospital visits, the medical costs for each visit, and survival. A frailty (random effects) Cox proportional hazards model is adopted to describe the recurrent hospital visits, using random effect u_i to capture the heterogeneity in the intensity of hospital visits. A random effects term v_i describes the heterogeneity in repeated measures of expenditures. The correlation between u_i and v_i specifies the relation between recurrent hospital visits and medical costs for each visit. Further, we assume that death hazard depends on repeated measures through v_i and recurrent events through u_i.

Denote the intensity function for recurrent hospital visits by $r_i\,(t)$. Denote the medical cost for the kth recurrent hospital visit as Y_{ik}. The joint model is written as:

$$r_i(t) = r_0(t)\exp(X_i^T\alpha + u_i) \quad \text{(D3-A)}$$

$$\log Y_{ik} = X_{ik}^T\beta + v_i + e_{ik} \quad \text{(D3-B)}$$

$$\lambda_i(t) = \lambda_0(t)\exp(X_i^T\delta + \eta_1 u_i + \eta_2 v_i) \quad \text{(D3-C)}$$

where $r_0(t)$ is the baseline intensity for recurrent hospital visits, and η_1 and η_2 are coefficients that specify the correlation among the three outcomes.

More recently, several papers extended the above model by incorporating more flexible functional forms and correlation structures, e.g., Sun et al. (2012), Zhao et al. (2014), Han et al. (2014), and Chen, Sun, and Liu (2015). Finally, application of the joint model is not limited to costs and mortality. It can be extended to include health reported outcomes, such as quality of life or health utilities.

E. Policy Implication

Longitudinal medical cost data can generate critical evidence to assist policy makers in resource allocation and coverage decisions by enhancing our understanding of the impact of health policies, interventions, or diseases on healthcare expenditures. Two types of studies using longitudinal medical costs data are especially helpful to policy makers: cost and utilization pattern from trend analysis, and estimates of the impact of a specific disease or condition on medical costs. Examples of each type of studies are provided below.

E.1. Trend Analysis

While methodological advances improve the quality of inference and mitigate potential biases in the analysis of longitudinal medical cost data, oftentimes descriptive analyses, such as trend analyses, are also necessary for a big-picture-type illustration. In the context of understanding the impact of new technology diffusion on medical costs, trends analyses are especially useful.

Geynisman et al. (2015) conducted trend analysis to evaluate the treatment patterns and associated costs in the United States as a result of treatment innovation in metastatic renal cell carcinoma (mRCC). Using data from the LifeLink Health Plan Claims Database, the study created a cohort of mRCC patients with at least 12 months of continuous enrollment from 2004 to 2011 and summarized treatment patterns as well as cost trend over time. A total of 1527 mRCC patients were analyzed. In 2010, nine unique treatment regimens were used for first-line treatment, 8 for second-line treatment, and 8 for third-line treatment. A significant association (odds ratio 1.26; $P < 0.001$) between the odds of advancing to third-line therapy or beyond and the number of targeted agents available was noted. For 767 patients receiving modern therapy who were < 65 years old, and stratifying by whether the first-line treatment was oral or intravenous, drug cost per patient with ancillary services was \$59,664 versus \$86,518, respectively ($P < 0.001$). Total costs and drug out-of-pocket costs per patient during the first year increased by the number of switches: \$111,680 to \$2355 for no switches, \$149,994 to \$2538 for 1 switch, and \$196,706 to \$3524 for 2 or more switches. In 2004, the median drug cost was \$11,458, while by 2010 it rose to \$68,660. The study concluded that a marked shift in the management of mRCC has occurred, with wide heterogeneity in treatment patterns.

Shih et al. (2015) examined the trends in costs and utilization of targeted therapeutics and the associated cost drivers among privately insured non-elderly cancer patients receiving chemotherapy. Using data from the 2001-2011 LifeLink™ Health Plan Claims Database, the study classified oncology drugs as targeted oral, targeted intravenous, and non-targeted anticancer medications, and reported disaggregated trends in utilization and in insurance and out-of-pocket payments per patient per month and during the first year of chemotherapy. This trend analysis found a large increase in the utilization of targeted intravenous anticancer medications and a gradual increase in targeted oral anticancer medications; targeted therapies accounts for 63% of all chemotherapy expenditures in 2011. Insurance payments per patient per month and in the first year of chemotherapy for targeted oral anticancer medications more than doubled in ten years, surpassing payments for targeted intravenous anticancer medications, which remained fairly constant throughout. Substitution towards targeted therapies and growth in drug prices both at launch and post-launch all contributed to payer spending growth. Out-of-pocket spending for targeted oral anticancer medications was half or less than the amount for targeted intravenous anticancer medications. Findings of this study offer strong evidence to policy makers to consider more aggressive management of pharmacy benefits for targeted oral anticancer medications and payment reforms for injectable drugs.

E.2. Impact of Disease on Cost

As discussed earlier, longitudinal medical cost data provide rich information for researchers to gain more insights on the dynamic interactions between disease on medical costs. Using data from the Clinical Data Repository at the University of Virginia Health System, Liu (2009) applied random effect two-part model to a cohort of patients with heart failure. Findings of this study are summarized below: (1) there is a significant increasing quadratic time effect happening 12 months after entry on the logit of probability of non-zero monthly costs ($p = 0.02$); (2) the visit time (from entry) has a quadratic pattern on monthly medical costs, which might be due to (i) high initial costs (because of initial diagnosis and treatment) and (ii) high end-of-life costs (because of intensive care for patients with terminal conditions); (3) there is no gender difference in both equations; (4) white patients tended to have a lower odds ratio (OR = 0.86, $p = 0.05$) of being treated in the hospital (or to have non-zero monthly medical costs). If they were treated, the monthly costs for white patients was lower (-0.234 in log scale, or 21% lower in a dollar value, $p = 0.002$). This reflects the fact that non-white patients had worse outcomes than white patients (Medscape report 2005); (5) elderly patients were more likely to have non-zero monthly medical costs (OR = 1.22 for every 10 years increase in age, $p < 0.0001$). However, age has a quadratic effect ($p = 0.002$) on the amount of positive monthly medical costs: it increases up to age 71, then decreases. There are two possible explanations for this decrease in monthly medical costs related to age: (a) older patients sought medical treatment more often, so monthly medical costs were diluted; and (b) older patients were usually treated less aggressively, thus incurred lower medical costs (Gatsonis et al. 1995). In addition, the study found that the estimates for the variance of both random effects are highly significant ($p < 0.0001$), which suggests the presence of within part correlation (i.e., the longitudinal outcomes of both cost being positive and the level of positive cost are correlated over time). Also, patients with higher odds of seeking medical care tended to incur more costs ($p < 0.0001$).

The flexible random effects two-part model developed by our research group (Liu et al. 2010) is well suited to estimate the impact of disease on medical costs in the presence of multiple years of claims data. Applied research using this method has surfaced in the literature, such as the study by Shojai et al. (2013).

E.3. Treatment Effect on Cost

We (Chen et al. 2015A) proposed a generalized partial linear single-index mixed models for analyzing repeated measures data. They applied the model to study the treatment effect of naltrexone on health costs in the multicenter COMBINE randomized controlled trial (Anton et al. 2006). Participants at 11 sites were randomized into 9 treatment groups. Eight of the treatment groups form a 2 × 2 × 2 factorial design in which patients were randomized to receive acamprosate (active or placebo), naltrexone (active or placebo), and either combined behavioral intervention (CBI) or no additional behavioral therapy. The ninth treatment group received only CBI. For illustration, we only consider treatment and placebo groups of naltrexone, where the treatment group includes naltrexone+CBI and naltrexone+NO CBI groups, and the placebo group includes placebo+CBI and placebo+NO CBI groups in the factorial design.

The health cost considered is the one year post treatment medical cost (Zarkin et al. 2010). The vector of baseline covariates include: age, gender, marriage, race, education, baseline costs covariates, and baseline drink. An indicator (0 for placebo and 1 for naltrexone) is used to denote treatment effect. We also account for the center effect by random effect. We are interested in the effect of naltrexone on health costs of alcohol-dependent individuals, adjusting for baseline covariates. The estimated linear coefficient for treatment indicator is negative, −0.312, and statistically significant (*P*-value = 0.031) using Wald test. It indicates that the individuals in the naltrexone group had lower post treatment health costs comparing with the placebo group.

E.4. Overview of Application of Research Related to MEPS Data

The MEPS, collected by Agency for Healthcare Research and Quality (AHRQ), is a probability sample designed to provide nationally representative estimates of health care use, medical expenditures, health attitudes, and health status in the U.S. civilian, non-institutionalized population (Cohen 2003). The researchers analyses will use the following files from the Household Component of the MEPS: the Full Year Consolidated data files (to obtain demographic and socioeconomic variables); Medical Condition file (to identify subgroups of patients with specific diseases, such as cancer), and Medical Event files (to obtain monthly medical costs from various medical events, such as hospitalization and office visits). All files can be linked via encrypted, unique person-identifiers.

E.4.1. Previous Research Findings related to MEPS

A unique and yet underexplored feature of the MEPS data is that it allows very comprehensive household- or dyad-level analyses because information on the majority of demographics, socioeconomic status, medical conditions, and health care utilization is available for every member who resides in the same household. We utilized this special feature of the MEPS data to examine the impact of cancer on families and constructed five cohorts from MEPS: individuals with a current diagnosis of cancer (CURR-F), individuals with no diagnosis of cancer who have a family member with a previous diagnosis of cancer (PREV-F), and individuals with no diagnosis of cancer in a family whose members have had no diagnosis of cancer (I-F).

We compared the rate of influenza vaccination among the aforementioned five groups of patients and family members, using data from the 2005 and 2006 MEPS (Shih and Pan 2010). We found that compared with the I-F group, the vaccination rate was substantially higher among patients with cancer and higher among non-cancer individuals in cancer families, although the latter association become insignificant in multivariate logistic regression. The results from this study suggest that the health condition of one person may affect the health behavior of his/her family members.

A similar pattern will likely be found in medical costs considering the financial constraints faced jointly by members of a family. It is possible that when one person in the family undergoes cancer treatment, other members of the family may delay or withhold medical care in order to avail most of the family resources to the cancer patient. Thus, the family members other than the cancer patient would incur lower medical costs. Using the cohorts of current cancer families constructed from MEPS, we compared the average monthly outpatient costs of current cancer patients and those of their non-cancer family members for five income classes: high-, middle-, low-income, near poor, and poor. Our preliminary analysis showed that although the cost pattern by income classes was mixed among cancer patients, there was a clear pattern of higher monthly outpatient costs among non-cancer individuals from the two highest income classes. These findings point to the importance of multilevel analyses in modeling longitudinal medical costs and reinforces the use of MEPS data to design their case studies.

E.4.2. Analysis of Correlated Medical Costs in MEPS

We (Chen et al. 2015B) developed a flexible model to analyze correlated medical costs in MEPS data. We constructed a subset of elderly households from the MEPS 2010 Full Year Consolidated Data File of the Household Survey, consisting of households in which every member was 65 years of age or over in the survey year. Using the elderly households as our study sample allows us to isolate the statistical issue to clustered medical costs without having to address additional analytical issues, such as massive zeros in medical costs (because very few elderly individuals would have zero medical expenditures) or endogeneity associated with choices of insurance (because Medicare eligibility starts at age 65, except for those with end-stage renal disease or disabled). The final study sample includes 2,139 individuals aged between 65 and 84 years within 1,556 households. Because age in MEPS is top coded at age 85, i.e., age over 85 is coded at 85, we choose the upper range as 84 to avoid erroneously attributing age effects of individuals over age 85 to those at 85.

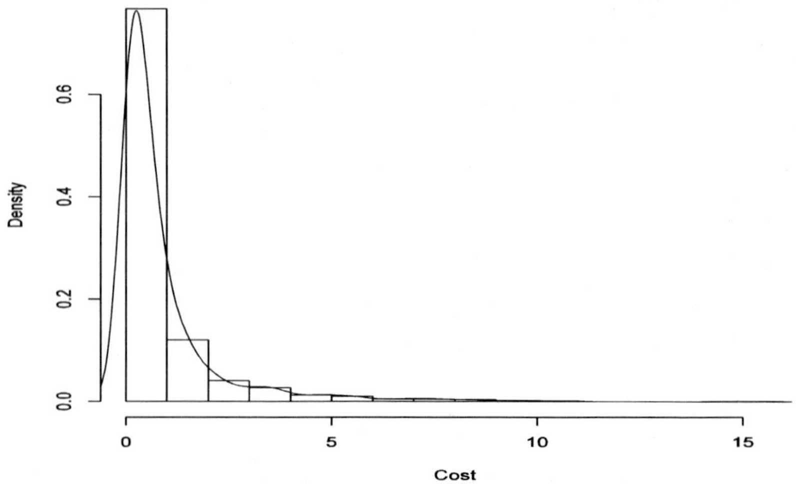

Figure 1. Histogram of Annual Medical Costs (in 1,000 U.S. dollars) for the MEPS data. The solid line is the estimated density.

The response variable in our model is annual medical costs in US dollars. Medical costs are highly skewed to the right (Figure 1), as is evident by a much larger mean (US \$9,235) than median (US \$3,955). Of the individuals in our study sample, the proportions for male, white race, having any hospitalization in the survey year, and death are 41.1%, 79.5%, 15.0%, and 1.4%, respectively. To account for the impact of an individual's underlying disease(s) on his/her medical costs, we consolidate 11 health high prevalence health conditions collected in the MEPS into five disease categories: heart and blood vessel disease (HBV, 82.7%), respiratory disease (16.9%), body movement disorder (76.6%), cancer (28.9%), diabetes (21.9%). Each disease category is quantified as dichotomous variable and included as a covariate in our analysis. There is a small portion (3.6%) of subjects who had no cost.

We apply a semiparametric model with exchangeable correlation to capture the possible correlation in medical costs for members within the same household. Specifically, the mean function of the model has the form:

$$\log(\mu_{ij}) = x_{ij}^T \beta + f(z_{ij}).$$

The covariate vector in the linear term x_{ij} includes 10 binary (1 for yes and 0 for no) predictors: male, white, death, hospitalization, each of the five disease categories, and a dichotomous variable indicating family composition (1 for family size greater than one, 0 for living alone). The continuous predictor in the nonlinear term z_{ij} is age.

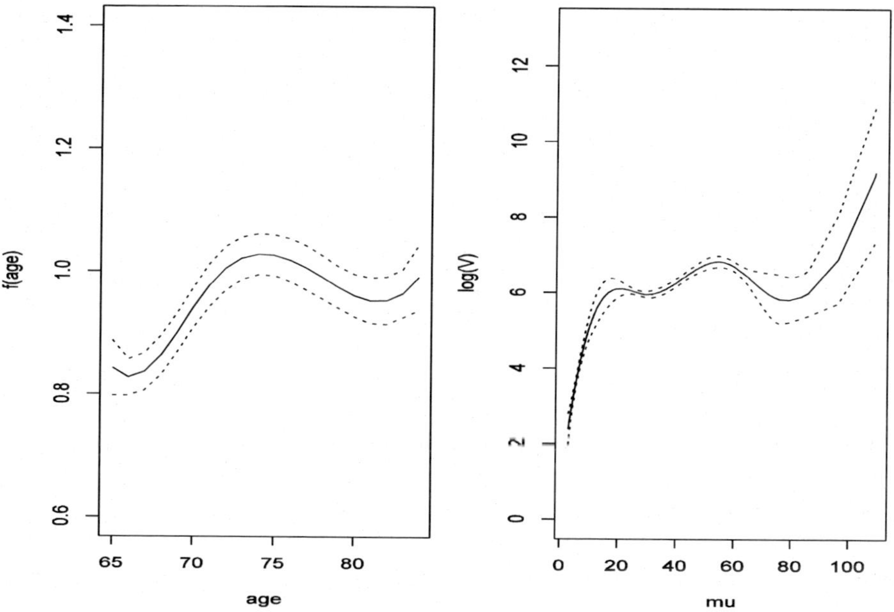

Figure 2. Curve Estimation for MEPS Data. Left: estimated $f(age)$ with 95% point-wise confidence interval; right: estimated variance function ("mu" represents the mean medical cost in the unit of US$1,000.

From the estimated coefficients $\hat{\beta}$, we find that gender and race are not significantly associated with annual medical costs, whereas significantly positive associations are observed between annual medical costs and death, hospitalization, and all five disease categories. Elderly living alone tended to have higher medical costs, although the effect is only marginally significant (P-value = 0.082). Such association can be explained by the fact that compared to those who live alone, elderly couples tend to take care of each other and thus reduce the need for home-based medical service or extended hospitalization due to the concern of unsafe home environment if patients were to be discharged home alone. The estimated correlation parameter is 0.041 and marginally significant (P-value = 0.062), suggesting elderly members in the same family share the similar medical spending pattern.

The estimated curve for age is shown in the left panel of Figure 2. We observe a nonlinear age effect on medical costs. There is a small dip at first, then the age effect increases from 67, reaches a maximum value around age 75 years, and fluctuates after 75. The small dip right after age 65 may reflect a tempered effect in healthcare utilization after a sharp increase in the use of medical services among those who were previously uninsured or underinsured before they became Medicare eligible at age 65. Medical costs then increases with age up to 75 as the health status deteriorates with age. After reaching age 75, patients might receive less aggressive treatment due to concerns of multiple chronic conditions so their costs fluctuates and do not exhibit a clearly increasing pattern. We also estimate the variance function as an unknown smooth function of mean. For this study, we observe a clear nonlinear curvature in the right panel of Figure 2 which indicates evidence of heteroscedasticity, as the variance increase with mean.

E.4.3. "Mapping" Studies in MEPS

Several studies have developed statistical algorithm to map the SF-12 to the EQ-5D preference index using the MEPS data. Development of such mapping algorithm is important because clinical trials and large survey often collect SF-12 information but not EQ-5D; thus, limiting the usefulness of data collected from these sources for cost-effectiveness analysis. A methodological challenge for such mapping studies is that data on health utilities are often bounded, have multiple modes, and a large proportion of observations clustered at values of "1." We contributed to the methodology in this research area by developing a finite mixture model that consists of a mixture to three distributions: a degenerate distribution with mass at values and two censored normal (also known as Tobit) distributions (Perraillon MC, Shih YCT, Thisted RA, 2015). The density of our proposed mixture model consists of two Tobit censored normal components and a degenerate distribution with mass at zero. This density is written as:

$$f(y)dy = \left[\sum_{j=1}^{2} \pi_j \frac{1}{\sigma_j} \emptyset\left(\frac{y - \mathbf{x}'_j \boldsymbol{\beta}_j}{\sigma_j}\right) dy\right]^{(1-d)} \left[\pi_0 + \sum_{j=1}^{2} \pi_j \, \Phi\left(-\frac{\mathbf{x}'_j \boldsymbol{\beta}_j}{\sigma_j}\right)\right]^{d},$$

where π_j are the mixture probabilities. Here, $\pi_0 = (1 - \pi_1 - \pi_2)$ is the mixture probability of the degenerate component.

Perraillon et al. (2015) applied this method to map the SF-12 to the EQ-5D preference index using the 2000 MEPS. The mapping algorithm is useful in situation in which information on health utilities is not available thus that researchers have to rely on condition-specific or generic measure of health status (e.g., SF-12) to predict or 'map' preferences. We split data in MEPS into estimation and validation samples to compare the prediction performance of our model to that of two previously developed methods: ordinary least squares (OLS) and two-part models.

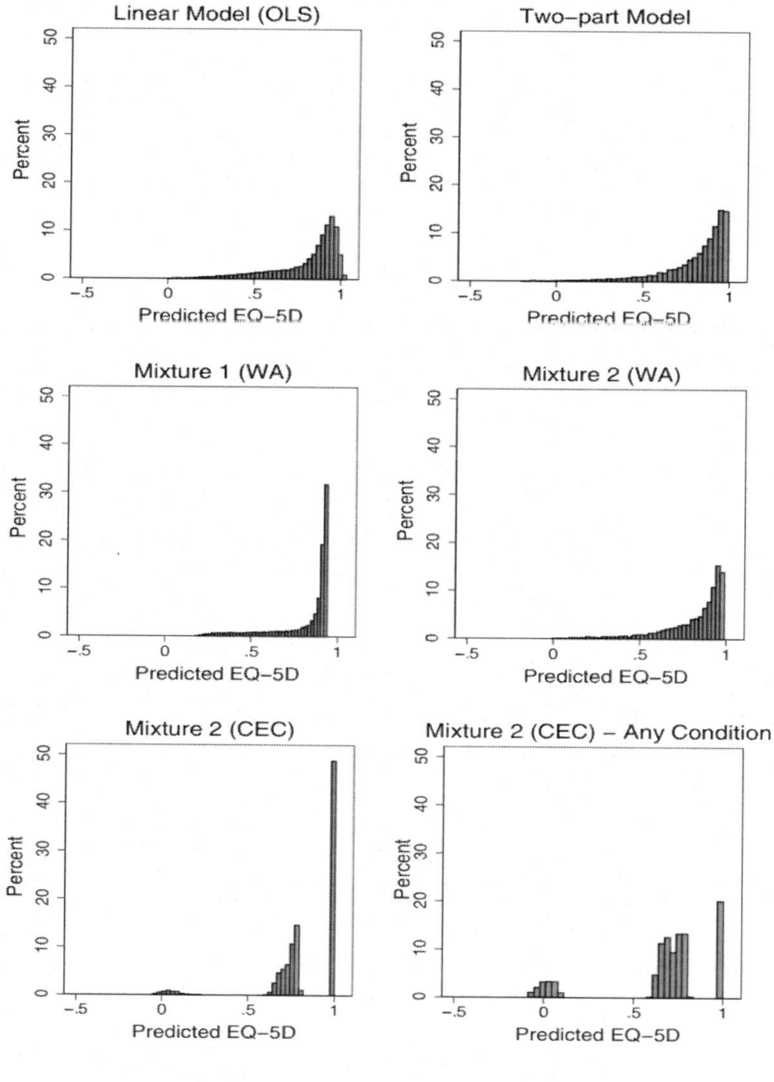

As shown, the finite mixture models outperform both two-part and OLS models. The study also found that the finite mixture models were most advantageous when applied to the subset with a large proportion of individuals not in good health. The study concluded that the use of mixture models is useful for researchers to obtain estimates of health utilities when only summary scores from the SF-12 and a limited number of demographic characteristics are available.

F. Discussion

This Chapter reviewed recent development in the statistical methodology of analyzing longitudinal medical costs data as well as outcomes data with unique distributional characteristics (e.g., skewness, clustering at value 0s). These methods not only allow more precise estimates of medical costs, but also produce more accurate projections of future costs. Such information is critical for policy makers in making budget allocation decision and also projecting the financial impact of diseases in the future.

Methods reviewed here can be expanded to separate cost increase driven by modifiable factors from those that are not modifiable. Modifiable factors are cost drivers that can be influenced or contained by policies or interventions. For example, use of expensive medical technologies that are not evidence-based can lead to increase in medical costs without achieving additional improvement in health benefits. Health insurance plans implementing reimbursement policies that discourage or decline payment for practice patterns that are not evidence based can potentially slow down the increase in medical costs without compromising healthcare quality. Conversely, non-modifiable factors are cost drivers that cannot be controlled via policies or interventions. For example, the aging of the US population is a demographic trend that cannot be reversed by any policies or medical interventions. Since age is one of the major risk factors for cancer, it is reasonable to expect that a proportion of increase in the cost of cancer care will be unavoidable due to the aging demographic in the US population. By isolating modifiable vs. non-modifiable factors in cost predictions, the comparison between different cost trajectories can inform policy makers of potential cost impact from policies or interventions targeted at modifiable factors; thus avoiding overly optimistic projection of policy impact.

REFERENCES

Anton, R. F., O'Malley, S. S., Ciraulo, D. A., Couper, D., Donovan, D. M., Gastfriend, D. R., Hosking, J. D., Johnson, B. A., LoCastro, J. S., Longabaugh, R., Mason, B. J., Mattson, M. E., Miller, W. R., Pettinati, H. M., Randall, C. L., Swift, R., Weiss, R. D.,Williams, L. D., and Zweben, A. (2006). Combined Pharmacotherapies and Behavioral Interventions for Alcohol Dependence—The COMBINE Study: A randomized Controlled Trial. *Journal of the American Medical Association* 295, 2003–2017.

Bang, H. and Tsiatis, A. (2000). Estimating medical costs with censored data. *Biometrika* 87, 329-343.

Bang, H., and Tsiatis, A. A. (2002). Median regression with censored cost data. *Biometrics* 58, 643-649.

Basu, A., and Rathouz, P. J. (2005). Estimating marginal and incremental effects on health outcomes using flexible link and variance function models. *Biostatistics* 6, 93-109.

Blough, D. K., Madden, C. W., and Hornbrook, M. C. (1999). Modeling risk using generalized linear models. *Journal of Health Economics* 18, 153-171.

Brown, M. L., Riley, G. F., Schussler, N., and Etzioni, R. (2002). Estimating health care costs related to cancer treatment from SEER-Medicare data. *Medical Care* 40, 104-117.

Buntin, M. B., and Zaslavsky, A. M. (2004). Too much ado about two-part models and transformation? Comparing methods of modeling Medicare expenditures. *Journal of Health Economics* 23, 525-542.

Chen, J., Liu, L., Zhang, D., and Shih, T. (2013A). A flexible model for the mean and variance functions, with application to medical cost data. *Statistics in Medicine* 32, 4306-4318.

Chen, J., Liu, L., Johnson, B. A., and O'Quigley, J. (2013B). Penalized likelihood estimation for semiparametric mixed models, with application to alcohol treatment research. *Statistics in Medicine.* 32, 335-46.

Chen, J., Kim, I., Terrell, G. R., Liu, L. (2015A). Generalized partial linear single-index mixed models for repeated measures data. *Journal of Nonparametric Statistics*. Accepted.

Chen, J., Liu, L., Shih, T., Zhang, D, Severini T. (2015B). A generalized partially linear marginal model with semiparametric covariance structure for correlated medical cost data. *Statistics in Medicine*. Under Revision.

Chen, X., Sun, J., Liu, L. (2015). Semiparametric partial linear quantile regression of longitudinal data with time-varying coefficients and informative observation times. *Statistica Sinica*. Accepted.

Cotter, D., Thamer, M., Narasimhan, K., Zhang, Y., and Bullock, K. (2006). Translating epoetin research into practice: The role of government and the use of scientific evidence. *Health Affairs* 25, 1249-59.

Cragg, J. G. (1971). Some statistical models for limited dependent variables with application to demand for durable goods. *Econometrica* 39, 829-844.

Diehr, P., Yanez, D., Ash, A., Hornbrook, M., and Lin, D. Y. (1999). Methods for analyzing health care utilization and costs. *Annual Review of Public Health* 20, 125-144.

Duan, N. (1983). Smearing estimate: a nonparametric retransformation method. *Journal of the American Statistical Association* 78, 605-610.

Duan, N., Manning, W. G., Morris, C., and Newhouse, J. P. (1983). A comparison of alternative models for the demand for medical care. *Journal of Business and Economic Statistics* 1, 115-126.

Etzioni, R., Riley, G. F., Ramsey, S. D., and Brown, M. (2002). Measuring costs - Administrative claims data, clinical trials, and beyond. *Medical Care* 40, 63-72.

Gatsonis, C. A., Epstein, A. M., Newhouse, J. P., Normand, S. L., and McNeil, B. J. (1995). Variations in the utilization of coronary angiography for elderly patients with an acute myocardial-infarction - an analysis using hierarchical logistic-regression. *Medical Care* 33, 625-642.

Geynisman DM, Hu JC, Liu L, Shih YCT. Treatment Patterns and Costs for Metastatic Renal Cell Carcinoma Patients with Private Insurance in the United States. *Clinical Genitourinary Cancer*. In Press.

Han, M., Song, X. Y., Sun, L., Liu, L. (2014). Joint modeling of longitudinal data with informative observation times and dropouts. *Statistica Sinica*. 24, 1487-1504.

Heitjan, D. F., Kim, C. Y., and Li, H. L. (2004). Bayesian estimation of cost-effectiveness from censored data. *Statistics in Medicine* 23, 1297-1309.

Jagsi R, Bekelman JE, Chen A, Chen RC, Hoffman K, Shih YC, Smith BD, Yu JB. (2014). Considerations for observational research using large data sets in radiation oncology. *Int J Radiat Oncol Biol Phys* 90, 11-24.

Kolata, G. 2012. Knotty challenges in health care costs. *The New York Times*, March 6, http://www.nytimes.com/2012/03/06/health/policy/an-interview-with-victor-fuchs-on-health-care-costs.html.

Lin, D. Y., Feuer, E. J., Etzioni, R., and Wax, Y. (1997). Estimating medical costs from incomplete follow-up data. *Biometrics* 53, 419-434.

Lin, D. Y., and Ying, Z. (2001). Semiparametric and nonparametric regression analysis of longitudinal data (with discussion). *Journal of the American Statistical Association* 96, 103-126.

Lin, H. Q., Scharfstein, D. O., and Rosenheck, R. A. (2004). Analysis of longitudinal data with irregular, outcome-dependent follow-up. *Journal of the Royal Statistical Society Series B* 66, 791-813.

Lipscomb J, Barnett PG, Brown ML, et al. (2009). Advancing the science of health care costing. *Medical Care* 47, S120-6.

Liu, L. (2009). Joint modeling longitudinal semi-continuous data and survival, with application to longitudinal medical cost data. *Statistics in Medicine* 28, 972-986.

Liu, L., Conaway, M. R., Knaus, W. A. and Bergin, J. (2008). A random effects four-part model, with application to correlated medical costs. *Computational Statistics and Data Analysis* 52, 4458-4473.

Liu, L., Huang, X. L., and O'Quigley, J. (2008). Analysis of longitudinal data in the presence of informative observational times and a dependent terminal event, with application to medical cost data. *Biometrics* 64, 950-958.

Liu, L., Strawderman, R., Cowen, M., and Shih, Y. (2010). A flexible two-part random effects model for correlated medical costs. *Journal of Health Economics* 29, 110-123.

Liu, L., Strawderman, R. L., Johnson, B. A., O'Quigley, J. M. (2015). Analyzing repeated measures semi-continuous data, with application to an alcohol dependence study. *Statistical Methods in Medical Research.* In press. doi: 10.1177/0962280212443324. PMID: 22474003.

Liu, L., Wolfe, R. A., and Kalbfleisch, J. D. (2007). A shared random effects model for censored medical costs and mortality. *Statistics in Medicine* 26, 139-155.

Lubitz, J., Cai, L. M., Kramarow, E., and Lentzner, H. (2003). Health, life expectancy, and health care spending among the elderly. *New England Journal of Medicine* 349, 1048-1055.

Manning, W. G., Morris, C. N., Newhouse, J. P., Orr, L. L., Duan, N., Keeler, E. B., Leibowitz, A., Marquis, K. H., Marquis, M. S. and Phelps, C. E. (1981). A two-part model of the demand for medical care: preliminary results from the health insurance study. In van der Gaag, J. and M. Perlman, eds., *Health, Economics, and Health Economics*. Leiden, The Netherlands: World Congress on Health Economis, pp.103-123.

Manning, W. G. (1998). The logged dependent variable, heteroscedasticity, and the retransformation problem. *Journal of Health Economics* 17, 283-295.

Manning, W. G., Basu, A., and Mullahy, J. (2005). Generalized modeling approaches to risk adjustment of skewed outcomes data. *Journal of Health Economics* 20, 465-488.

Manning, W. G., and Mullahy, J. (2001). Estimating log models: to transform or not to transform? *Journal of Health Economics* 20, 461-494.

McCullagh, P. and Nelder, J. A. (1989). *Generalized Linear Models*, 2 edn, London: Chapman and Hall.

Medscape, 2005. Evidence-based medical therapy and device therapy for heart failure: Points of emphasis in the New 2005 AHA/ACC guidelines. Available at: http://www.medscape.com/viewarticle/520123.

Mullahy, J. (1998). Much ado about two: reconsidering retransformation and the two-part model in health econometrics. *Journal of Health Economics* 17, 247-281.

Obama, B. (2009). Remarks by the president on reforming the health care system to reduce costs. Released from the Office of the Press Secretary, The White House, May 11, 2009. Available at http://www.whitehouse.gov/the_press_office/Remarks-by-the-President-on-Reforming-the-Health-Care-System-to-Reduce-Costs/.

Olsen, M. K., and Schafer, J. L. (2001). A two-part random effects model for semicontinuous longitudinal data. *Journal of the American Statistical Association* 96, 730-745.

Orszag, P. (2009). Medicare trustees to America: Bend the curve! Statements released from the Office of Management and Budget, The White House, May 12, 2009. Available at http://www.whitehouse.gov/omb/blog/09/05/12/MedicareTrusteestoAmericaBendtheCurve/.

Perraillon MC, Shih YCT, Thisted RA. Predicting the EQ 5D 3L Preference Index from the SF-12 Health Survey in a National US Sample: A Finite Mixture Approach. *Medical Decision Making*. In Press.

Ruppert, D., Wand, M. P., and Carroll, R. J. (2003). Semiparametric Regression. New York: Cambridge University Press.

Shih YCT, Smieliauskas F, Geynisman DM, Kelly RJ, Smith TJ. Trends in the costs and utilization of targeted cancer therapies for the privately insured non-elderly: 2001-2011. *Journal of Clinical Oncology*. In Press.

Shih YCT, Pan IW. Influenza Vaccination among Individuals with Cancer and Their Family Members. *American Journal of Preventive Medicine*. 2010; 38(1): 61-69.

Shojai M, Kazemnejad A, Zayeri F, Vahedi M. Application of semi-parametric single-index two-part regression and parametric two-part regression in estimation of the cost of functional gastrointestinal disorders. *Gastroenterol Hepatol Bed Bench*. 2013 Fall; 6(4):202-9.

Sisko, A., Truffer, C., Smith, S., et al. (2009). Health spending projections through 2018: recession effects add uncertainty to the outlook. *Health Affairs* 28, W346-W357.

Stearns, S. C., and Norton, E. C. (2004). Time to include time to death? The future of health care expenditure predictions. *Health Economics* 13, 315-327.

Sun, J. G., Park, D. H., Sun, L. Q., and Zhao, X. Q. (2005). Semiparametric regression analysis of longitudinal data with informative observation times. *Journal of the American Statistical Association* 100, 882-889.

Sun, L., Song, X., Zhou, J. and Liu, L. (2012). Joint analysis of longitudinal data with informative observation times and a dependent terminal event. *Journal of American Statistical Association: Theory and Method* 107, 688-700.

Sun, Z., Liu, L., Shih, YCT (2015). A new local likelihood kernel estimation method for semi-parametric partial linear random effects models. Submitted.

Tooze, J. A., Grunwald, G. K. and Jones, R. H. (2002). Analysis of repeated measures data with clumping at zero. *Statistical Methods in Medical Research* 11, 341-355.

Yabroff, K. R., Warren, J. L., Schrag, D., et al. (2009). Comparison of approaches for estimating incidence costs of care for colorectal cancer patients. *Medical Care* 47, Suppl 1, S56-S63.

Zarkin, G. A., Gray, J. W., Aldridge, A., Mills, M., Cisler, R. A., Couper, D., McKay, J. R., and O'Malley S. (2010). The Effect of Alcohol Treatment on Social Costs of Alcohol Dependence Results from the COMBINE Study. *Medical Care*. 48, 396–401.

Zhao X., Deng S., Liu L., Liu, L. (2014). Sieve estimation in semiparametric modeling of longitudinal data with informative observation times. *Biostatistics*. 15, 140-153.

In: Health Care Costs
Editor: Brandon Hill

ISBN: 978-1-63484-619-6

Chapter 2

APPLICATION OF DA VINCI® ROBOT IN GENERAL SURGERY: A COST ASSESSMENT

Ioannis D. Gkegkes[1] and Christos Iavazzo[2]
[1]First Department of Surgery,
General Hospital of Attica "KAT," Athens, Greece
[2]Gynaecological Oncology Department, Christie Hospital,
Manchester, UK

ABSTRACT

The utilization of robotic assisted surgical techniques represents a novelty in the field of general surgery. Moreover, the development of robotic technology facilitated the realization of complex operations both in hepatopancreatic and in colorectal surgery. However, the elevated costs of the robotic assisted surgery, in comparison to the other minimally invasive procedures, mainly the laparoscopic ones, make the application of robotics in general surgery expensive and not an everyday surgical technique. The present evidence reveals that robotic surgery, under specific conditions, has the potential to become cost-effective. Large number of cases, presence of industry competition and multidisciplinary team utilization are some of the factors that could make more reasonable and cost-effective the robotic assisted technique.

The evolution of robotic technology applications in surgery during the last decade has facilitated the realization of a great variety of operations in various surgical fields [1]. The robotic assisted technique has an important position among the other minimally invasive methods in general surgery. Several are the main advantages of robotic assisted surgery, such as three dimensional view of the operating field, low intraoperative blood loss, precision of movements due to elimination of surgeon tremor, utilization of wristed instruments that improve dexterity and facilitate suturing, have made possible even the most complicate operations such as robotic pancreaticoduodenectomy [2-4]. In contrast to the above mentioned advantages, the absence of tactile feedback of the surgeon and the cost are the main weak points of the robotic technique.

Nowadays, the only commercially available robotic equipment (da Vinci® Surgical System) is characterized by elevated cost, including cost of acquisition, training and equipment-instrument cost, as well as that of maintenance of the robotic system (with an annual service contract, over 100,000 US dollars). This high cost can explain the reasons that decreased the widespread use of robotic assisted surgery [4]. According to van Dam et al., in order to amortize the initial capital for the acquisition of robotic devices, the technique should be applied on more than 300 surgical procedures per year for a period longer of 7 years, equivalent to an amount of over 1,000 Euros per patient [4]. As a result, it can be easily understood that the robotic technology refers exclusively to surgical centers with large volume of patients in order to achieve the per case charges as low as possible. The robotic instrumentation that has increased cost of acquisition (almost over 1,500 Euros per instrument) as well as a limited number of uses (10 lives per instrument) represents another financial burden [5]. Moreover, the reimbursement to the hospital for utilization of the robot is in direct correlation with the type of health insurance and the health system itself, favoring the countries without universal health coverage

The introduction of innovative and less invasive technologies in surgical fields has been adopted with great difficulty from the health care systems as a consequence of the lack of data and of the high costs (acquisition and maintenance) of every novel equipment [6]. In the current finance situation, where the major part of the European economies and a portion of the rest of the world are facing difficulties to sustain the already present health structures, doubts could be raised in the attempts to introduce new and highly expensive technique such as robotics as the new standard of care without the presence of strong evidence of significant cost effectiveness and the comparison of minimally invasive methods to standard surgical techniques. Though cost related studies are complicated to be organized, it is essential that all parts involved, society and doctors, should comprehend the impact of the cost of robotics.

Robotic assisted surgery specifically requires equipment of elevated cost as result of the novelty and the high specialization of the utilized devices [5, 7]. The high cost of acquisition (over 1 million Euros) as well the expensive maintenance costs (almost 150,000 Euros /year) are obstacles that should be overcome. Van Dam et al. has suggested that the costs of robotic equipment could be amortized, if the health care systems permit the application of robotic equipment on elevated number of patients [4]. Furthermore, the absence of competition in the market of robotic equipment, especially after 2003, is one of the most important factors that maintain high the costs of robotic instrumentation [8]. More specifically, in 2003, the merge of the only two existed companies in the market of robotic devices was achieved, creating monopoly conditions.

The operating time is another essential reason that may cause great variations on the total surgical costs. Even though for private health structures the length of the operating time is not an issue, for public health systems, which are financed by the government's budget, every penny must be carefully spent. The setup of the robotic equipment, which is significantly longer compared to either the laparoscopic or the open one can increase the cost, however, it was shown that this time can be substantially improved when the surgical team is well trained [6]. Furthermore, the operative time is related to the experience of the surgical team. The type of surgical operation, as well as the surgeon's capability and experience are factors that influence considerably the learning curve [4]. In addition, the costs are in correlation with the learning curve and are considered as an additional cost caused by the fact that surgeons already went through a training program for both laparoscopic and open technique [9]. Nevertheless, it should be mentioned that an effective way to decrease the costs related to learning curve is the presence of great volume of patients and the necessity of virtual reality simulators [10, 11].

Minimal invasive techniques have revealed to have an edge over laparotomy for the management of patients in a wide spectrum of pathologies [12, 13]. Keyhole incisions offer various advantages over the open surgical method, such as decrease of both post-operative pain and recovery time, less post operative complications, reduced blood loss, better cosmetic result. In particular, robotic techniques have a positive impact on specific patients' categories, such as the reduction of operative costs and of hospital stay in elderly or morbidly obese patients. According to some studies, the total cost between both open and laparoscopic technique do not present statistically significant difference [14, 15].

The extent of hospital stay has an important influence on the total charges of hospitalization. The limited hospital stay is a principal characteristic of both robotic and laparoscopic approach as it is expected in comparison to the open method [5]. Therefore, the decreased number of hospital days can amortize part of the increased operative costs of the minimal invasive techniques. Besides, the expenses of hospitalization are also in strait correlation with the category of health care system and the type of health care structure [4, 16]. Differences between countries, private or public sectors render complex any approach in order to evaluate those cost data. Regarding the comparison of robotic procedures to laparoscopy, several studies claim that over hospital stay the robotic surgery seems to have a slight financial advantage over the standard laparoscopy [17]. Nevertheless, currently, it appears that laparoscopy is a most economic approach among the other minimal invasive methods.

As presented in Table 1, the greater part of the studies referred to gastric fundoplication and showed that robotic is more expensive in comparison to laparoscopic technique. Despite the cost of acquisiting the robotic devices, professional charges, operating room costs, surgical equipment costs present great variation in the included studies. Such a cost could be minimized if we also take into consideration the decrease of the hospital stay, the sooner return to normal patient's activities, the reduction of blood loss and the decrease on conversion rates to laparotomy. Also, by improving the robotic training of all personnel, the surgical time could be further reduced and as consequence favor the use of minimal invasive techniques.

The utilization of robotics in almost every surgical field could be thought, in the future, as a valuable tool in common surgical practice. In order to realize this fact, both operative costs and unnecessary charges should be eliminated. The formation of specialized robotic units operating on great number of cases per year, the reduction of operating time per procedure by specialized training on robotic approach, the decision for early discharge of the patients when that is possible and the minimization of the number of instruments used per operation are some of the first steps that could be done in this direction. An additional proposal to minimize the cost is the multiple-use of the robotic equipment by multiple surgical specialties, good training of all the team members implicated while the acquisition of the robotic devices could be made through research funding or even charities.

Table 1. Robotics in general surgery: costs related to equipment and peri-operative outcomes[†]

First author, Year [ref]	Type of operation	Number of patients (%)	Total costs	Operative charges	Non-operative charges	Robot cost included	Surgical equipment costs	Operating room costs	Length of hospital stay (days)	Conversion to laparo-tomy (%)	Duration of surgery (min)	Blood loss (mL)
Adhesiolysis												
Salman, 2013 [18]	OP	165,078/226,445 (16.3)	median[‡]: 32,020	NR	NR	NR	NR	NR	median[‡]: 5.7	NR	NR	NR
	LA	205,813/1,162,790 (17.7)	median[‡]: 30,318	NR	NR		NR	NR	median[‡]: 4.7	NR	NR	NR
	RO	34,177/37,270 (91.7)	median[‡]: 21,995 $p < 0.05$	NR	NR		NR	NR	median[‡]: 4.9 $p < 0.05$	NR	NR	NR
Adrenalectomy												
Salman, 2013 [18]	OP	16,530/226,445 (7.3)	median[‡]: 39,692	NR	NR	NR	NR	NR	median[‡]: 6.7	NR	NR	NR
	LA	3,488/1,162,790 (0.3)	median[‡]: 31,207	NR	NR		NR	NR	median[‡]: 6.2	NR	NR	NR
	RO	447/37,270 (1.2)	median[‡]: 32,712 $p < 0.05$	NR	NR		NR	NR	median[‡]: 6.7 $p < 0.05$	NR	NR	NR
Brunaud, 2008 [19]	LA	-	mean: 1,799	NR	NR	NR	NR	NR	NR	NR	NR	NR
	RO	100	mean: 4,102	NR	NR		NR	NR	mean (SD): 6.4 (3)	5/100 (5)	mean (SD) (range): 99 (35) (40-275)	NR
Prewitt, 2008 [20]	OP	-	NR	NR	NR	NR	NR	NR	-	NR	NR	NR
	RO	16	NR	mean: 6,942	NR		NR	NR	mean: 1.8	NR	NR	NR

Table 1. (Continued)

First author, Year [ref]	Type of operation	Number of patients (%)	Total costs	Operative charges	Non-operative charges	Robot cost included (Y/N)	Surgical equipment costs	Operating room costs	Length of hospital stay (days)	Conversion to laparo-tomy (%)	Duration of surgery (min)	Blood loss (mL)
Winter, 2006 [21]	OP	20/95 (21)	median: 13,383	median: 2,686	median: 10,697	NR	NR	NR	-	NR	NR	NR
	LA	45/95 (47)	median: 13,197	median: 4,699	median: 8,498		NR	NR	median: 2	4/45 (9)	NR	NR
	RO	30/95 (32)	median: 15,842	median: 6,334	median: 9,508		NR	NR	median: 2	0/30	median (range): 185 (130-295)	NR
Morino, 2004 [22]	LA	10/20 (50)	mean: 2,005	mean: 1,027	mean: 991	N	mean: 598	mean: 428	mean (range): 5.4 (4-8)	0/10	mean (range): 115.3 (95-155)	NR
	RO	10/20 (50)	mean: 2,539 $p < 0.01$	mean: 1,510	mean: 1,046		mean: 873	mean: 636	mean (range): 5.7 (4-9) p = NS	4/10 (40)	mean (range): 169 (136-215) $p < 0.01$	NR
Adjustable gastric banding												
Muehlmann, 2003 [23]	LA	10/20 (50)	NR	mean: 4,587	NR	NR	NR	NR	mean (range): 3 (2-4)	NR	mean (range): 97 (60-140)	NR
	RO	10/20 (50)	NR	mean: 6,964 $p<0.001$	NR		mean: 1,089	NR	mean (range): 3 (2-4)	NR	mean (range): 137 (110-175) $p = 0.04$	NR

First author, Year [ref]	Type of operation	Number of patients (%)	Total costs	Operative charges	Non-operative charges	Robot cost included	Surgical equipment costs	Operating room costs	Length of hospital stay (days)	Conversion to laparo-tomy (%)	Duration of surgery (min)	Blood loss (mL)
Cholecystectomy												
Buzat, 2013 [24]	LA	10/30 (33)	NR	NR	NR	N	mean: 945	NR	NR	0/10	mean (SD): 85.5 (11.8)	mean (SD): 12 (7.5)
	RO	20/30 (67)	NR	NR	NR		mean: 935	NR	NR	0/20	mean (SD): 84.6 (20.5) p = 0.8737	mean (SD): 8.4 (7.3) p=0.2289
Salman, 2013 [18]	OP	NA	NA	NR	NR	NR	NR	NR	NA	NR	NR	NR
	LA	731,395/1,162,790 (62.9)	median‡: 23,561	NR	NR		NR	NR	median‡: 4.1	NR	NR	NR
	RO	484/37,270 (1.3)	median‡: 23,307	NR	NR		NR	NR	median‡: 4.4	NR	NR	NR
Breitenstein, 2008 [25]	LA	50/100 (50)	mean (SD): 4,583 (1,433)	mean: 1,223	mean: 3,390	Y	NR	NR	mean (SD): 4.84 (2.2)	0/50	mean (SD): 50.2 (29.2)	NR
	RO	50/100 (50)	mean (SD): 5,851 (1,290)	mean: 1,291	mean: 4,598		NR	NR	mean (SD): 4.58 (1.9) p = 0.4	0/50	mean (SD): 54.6 (31.6) p = 0.54	NR
Heemskerk, 2005 [26]	LA	12/24 (50)	mean: 2,148.45	mean: 273.74	mean: 1,874.71	Y	-	NR	mean: 2.3	0/12	mean: 1.30 ††	NR
	RO	12/24 (50)	mean: 3,329.07 p < 0.001	mean: 1,163.75	mean: 2,165.32		mean: 889.18 p < 0.001	NR	mean: 2.7 p = 0.208	0/12	mean: 1.55 †† p = 0.17	NR

Table 1. (Continued)

First author, Year [ref]	Type of operation	Number of patients (%)	Total costs	Operative charges	Non-operative charges	Robot cost included (Y/N)	Surgical equipment costs	Operating room costs	Length of hospital stay (days)	Conversion to laparotomy (%)	Duration of surgery (min)	Blood loss (mL)
Colectomy												
Keller, 2013 [27]	LA	17,265/18,009 (95.9)	mean: 31,970	mean: 2,571	mean: 29,399	Y	mean: 2,252	NR	mean: 6.13	0/17,265	mean: 201	NR
	RO	744//18,009 (4.1)	mean: 39,160	mean: 3,572 $p < 0.001$	mean: 35,588		mean: 3,777 $p < 0.001$	NR	mean: 7.46 $p < 0.001$	0/744	mean: 261 $p < 0.001$	NR
Park, 2012 [28]	LA	35/70 (50)	mean (SD): 7,561 (1,178)	mean: 5,014	mean: 2,596	Y	mean (SD): 4,468 (4,091)	NR	mean (SD): 8.3 (4.2)	0/35	mean (SD): 130 (43)	mean (SD): 56.8 (31.3)
	RO	35/70 (50)	mean (SD): 8,964 (1,398) $p = 0.013$	mean: 7,451	mean: 1,572		mean (SD): 6,639 (979) $p < 0.001$	NR	mean (SD): 7.9 (4.1) $p = 0.13$	0/35	mean (SD): 195 (41) $p < 0.001$	mean (SD): 35.8 (26.3) $p = 0.211$
Bertani, 2011 [29]	OP	45/109 (41.3)	mean: 7,888	NR	NR	Y	mean: 1,694	mean: 795	median (range): 6 (5-32)	-	median (range): 133 (55-210)	median (range): 150 (50-500)
	LA	30/109 (27.5)	mean: 7,968	NR	NR		mean: 2,066	mean: 1,128	median (range): 5 (3-12)	2/30 (6.7)	median (range): 210 (150-	median (range): 110 (50-

First author, Year [ref]	Type of operation	Number of patients (%)	Total costs	Operative charges	Non-operative charges	Robot cost included	Surgical equipment costs	Operating room costs	Length of hospital stay (days)	Conversion to laparotomy (%)	Duration of surgery (min)	Blood loss (mL)
									$p < 0.001$**		360) $p < 0.001$**	300)
	RO	34/109 (31.2)	mean: 10,027	NR	NR		mean: 3,166	mean: 1,011	median (range): 5 (4-17)	2/34 (5.9)	median (range): 194 (130-301) $p < 0.001$*	median (range): 170 (80-1,000)
de Souza, 2010 [30]	LA	135/175 (77.1)	median (range): 9,057 (5,712-58,203)	median (range): 5,458 (3,109-33,865)	median (range): 3,739 (2,248-24,339)	NR	NR	NR	median (range): 5 (2-16)	1/135 (0.74)	mean (SD): 118.08 (38.11)	median (range): 50 (100-600)
	RO	40/175 (22.9)	median (range): 11,131 (7,181-28,173) $p = 0.003$	median (range): 6,816 (3,739-17,080) $p = 0.004$	median (range): 4,556 (3,442-11,093) $p = 0.003$		NR	NR	median (range): 5 (3-10) $p=0.861$	1/40 (2.5) $p=0.402$	mean (SD): 158.93 (36.69) $p<0.001$	median (range): 50 (10-240) $p=0.52$
Rawlings, 2007 [31]	LA	15/32 (46.9)	mean (SD): 5,954 (2,069)	NR	NR	NR	mean (SD): 1,358 (382)	mean (SD): 3,200 (639)	mean (SD): 5.5 (3.4)	2/15 (13.3)	mean (SD): 169.2 (37.5)	mean (SD): 66.3 (50.7)
	RO	17/32 (53.1)	mean (SD): 6,825 (3,743) $p = 0.43$	NR	NR		mean (SD): 2,176 (350) $p < 0.0001$	mean (SD): 4,294 (669) $p < 0.0001$	mean (SD): 5.2 (5.8) $p = 0.862$	0/17	mean (SD): 218.9 (44.6) $p = 0.002$	mean (SD): 40 (24.9) $p = 0.067$

Table 1. (Continued)

First author, Year [ref]	Type of operation	Number of patients (%)	Total costs	Operative charges	Non-operative charges	Robot cost included	Surgical equipment costs	Operating room costs	Length of hospital stay (days)	Conversion to laparotomy (%)	Duration of surgery (min)	Blood loss (mL)
Sigmoidectomy												
Rawlings, 2007 [31]	LA	12/25 (48)	mean (SD): 7,889 (8,642)	NR	NR	NR	mean (SD): 1,650 (698)	mean (SD): 3,668 (1,177)	mean (SD): 6.6 (8.3)	0/12	mean (SD): 199.4 (44.5)	mean (SD): 65.4 (52.1)
	RO	13/25 (52)	mean (SD): 9,097 (8,969) p=0.735	NR	NR		mean (SD): 2,330 (470) p=0.003	mean (SD): 4,468 (903) p=0.0 68	mean (SD): 6.0 (7.3) p=0.854	2/13 (15.4)	mean (SD): 225.2 (37.1) p=0.128	mean (SD): 90.4 (60) p=0.28
Rectal resection												
Baek, 2012 [32]	LA	150/304 (49.3)	mean (SD): 7,311 (2,600)	mean (SD): 1,677 (430)	mean: 5,634	Y	mean (SD): 2,457 (544)	NR	mean (SD): 10.8 (8.6)	NR	mean (SD): 219.7 (71.2)	mean (SD): 126.2 (267.7)
	RO	154/304 (50.7)	mean (SD): 10,731 (2,800) p = 0.001	mean (SD): 6,483 (1,167) p < 0.001	mean: 4,248		mean (SD): 644 (7,194) p < 0.001	NR	mean (SD): 11.1 (7.0) p = 0.819	NR	mean (SD): 285.2 (69.1) p = 0.018	mean (SD): 167.8 (26.1) p = 0.2
Bertani, 2011 [29]	OP	34/86 (39.5)	mean: 9,858	NR	NR	Y	mean: 2,511	mean: 954	median (range): 7 (4-24)	0/34	median (range): 164 (100-350)	median (range): 120 (50-2,000)

First author, Year [ref]	Type of operation	Number of patients (%)	Total costs	Operative charges	Non-operative charges	Robot cost included (Y/N)	Surgical equipment costs	Operating room costs	Length of hospital stay (days)	Conversion to laparotomy (%)	Duration of surgery (min)	Blood loss (mL)
	RO	52/86 (60.5)	mean: 11,214	NR	NR		mean: 3,140	mean: 1,417	median (range): 6 (4-51) $p = 0.004$	2/52 (4)	median (range): 260 (190-370) $p = 0.001$	median (range): 100 (50-1,000) $p = 0.146$
Gastroenterostomy												
Wormer, 2013 [33]	LA	29,677/29,959 (99.1)	mean (SD): 31,317 (17,120)	NR	NR	NR	NR	NR	mean (SD): 2.2 (1.5)	NR	NR	NR
	RO	282/29,959 (0.9)	mean (SD): 44,574 (21,165) $p < 0.05$	NR	NR		NR	NR	mean (SD): 2.5 (2.4) $p < 0.05$	NR	NR	NR
Fundoplication												
Owen, 2014 [34]	OP	2,168/ 12,079 (18)	mean (SD): 9,353 (10,244) $p < 0.05$**	NR	NR	NR	NR	NR	mean (SD): 6.1 (7.2) $p < 0.05$**	NR	NR	NR
	LA	9,572/12,079 (79.2)	mean (SD): 5,838 (5106) $p < 0.05$***	NR	NR		NR	NR	mean (SD): 2.8 (3.6) p = NS***	NR	NR	NR
	RO	339/12,079 (2.8)	mean (SD): 7,799 (4,426) $p < 0.05$*	NR	NR		NR	NR	mean (SD): 3 (3.5) $p < 0.05$*	NR	NR	NR

Table 1. (Continued)

First author, Year [ref]	Type of operation	Number of patients (%)	Total costs	Operative charges	Non-operative charges	Robot cost included (Y/N)	Surgical equipment costs	Operating room costs	Length of hospital stay (days)	Conversion to laparotomy (%)	Duration of surgery (min)	Blood loss (mL)
Wormer, 2013 [33]	LA	7,484/7,756 (96.5)	mean (SD): 24,139 (17,622)	NR	NR	NR	NR	NR	mean (SD): 2.3 (2)	NR	NR	NR
	RO	272/7,756 (3.5)	mean (SD): 27,576 (15,484) $p < 0.05$	NR	NR		NR	NR	mean (SD): 2.3 (2)	NR	NR	NR
Nakadi, 2010 [35]	LA	11/20 (55)	mean (SEM):5,907 (168)	mean (SEM): 1,525 (35)	mean: 4,382	N	mean: 76	NR	mean (SEM): 4.1 (0.3)	0/11	mean (SEM): 96 (5)	NR
	RO	9/20 (45)	mean (SEM): 27,561 (99) $p < 0.001$	mean (SEM): 1,553 (40) $p = 0.601$	mean: 26,008		mean: 1,214 $p < 0.001$	NR	mean (SEM): 4.4 (0.2) $p = 0.284$	1/9 (11.1)	mean (SEM): 137 (12) $p = 0.01$	NR
Andeberg, 2009 [36]	OP	10/34 (29.4)	mean: 10,521	NR	mean: 8,347	N	NR	NR	mean (SD): 7.9 (2.8)	NR	mean (SD): 129 (43)	NR
	LA	10/34 (29.4)	mean: 8,982	NR	mean: 5,494		NR	NR	mean (SD): 5.2 (3.0)	2/10 (20)	mean (SD): 207 (52)	NR
	RO	14/34 (41.2)	mean: 9,584	NR	mean: 4,015		mean: 2,081	NR	mean (SD): 3.8 (1.9) $p=0.002$	NR	mean (SD): 207 (47) $p=0.003$	NR

First author, Year [ref]	Type of operation	Number of patients (%)	Total costs	Operative charges	Non-operative charges	Robot cost included (Y/N)	Surgical equipment costs	Operating room costs	Length of hospital stay (days)	Conversion to laparotomy (%)	Duration of surgery (min)	Blood loss (mL)
Heemskerk, 2007 [37]	LA	11/22 (50)	mean: 3,376.35	NR	NR	NR	NR	NR	mean: 4	0/11	mean: 135	NR
	RO	11/22 (50)	mean: 4,363.82 p = 0.033	NR	NR		NR	NR	mean: 4 p=0.928	0/11	mean: 176 p=0.094	NR
Mueller-Stich, 2007 [38]	LA	20/40 (50)	mean (SD): 2,743 (483)	mean (SD): 763 (115)	NR	NR	NR	NR	mean (SD): 3.3 (0.8)	0/40	mean (SD): 102 (19)	NR
	RO	20/40 (50)	mean (SD): 3,244 (512) p = 0.03	mean (SD): 1,534 (111) p=0.001	NR		NR	NR	mean (SD): 2.9 (0.8) p=0.086	0/40	mean (SD): 88 (18) p=0.033	NR
Morino, 2006 [39]	LA	25/50 (50)	mean: 1,527	mean: 657	mean: 870	N	mean: 100	mean: 557	mean (range): 2.9 (2-6)	0/25	mean (SEM): 91.1 (10.6)	NR
	RO	25/50 (50)	mean: 3,157 p<0.001	mean: 2,257	mean: 900		mean: 1,454	mean: 803	mean (range): 3 (2-7) p=0.588	1/25 (4)	mean (SEM): 131.3 (18.3) p<0.001	NR
Pancreatectomy												
Kang, 2011 [40]	LA	25/45 (55.6)	mean (SD): 2,829 (1,263)	mean (SD): 1,628 (460)	NR	Y	NR	NR	mean (SD): 7.3 (3.0)	NR	mean (SD): 258.2 (118.6)	mean (SD): 420.2 (445.5)
	RO	20/45 (44.4)	mean (SD): 6,085 (637) p < 0.001	mean (SD): 4,215 (279) p < 0.001	NR		NR	NR	mean (SD): 7.1 (2.2) p = NS	NR	mean (SD): 328.7 (121.8) p = 0.024	mean (SD): 372 (341.5) p = NS

Table 1. (Continued)

First author, Year [ref]	Type of operation	Number of patients (%)	Total costs	Operative charges	Non-operative charges	Robot cost included (Y/N)	Surgical equipment costs	Operating room costs	Length of hospital stay (days)	Conversion to laparotomy (%)	Duration of surgery (min)	Blood loss (mL)
Waters, 2010 [41]	OP	22/57 (38.6)	mean: 11,372	mean: 2,572	mean: 8,800	Y	NR	NR	mean (range): 8 (3-25)	-	mean (range): 234 (136-437)	mean (range): 681 (50-3,300)
	LA	18/57 (31.6)	mean: 9,451	mean: 2,251	mean: 7,201		NR	NR	mean (range): 6 (3-34)	2/18 (11.1)	mean (range): 224 (100-346)	mean (range): 667 (50-7,000)
	RO	17/57 (29.8)	mean: 7,758	mean: 3,589 p = 0.04	mean: 4,169 p = 0.01		NR	NR	mean (range): 4 (2-6) p=0.04	2/17 (11.7)	mean (range): 298 (191-418) p=0.01	mean (range): 279 (20-1,200) p=0.17
Rectopexy												
Heemskerk, 2007 [42]	LA	14/33 (42.4)	mean: 3,115.55	NR	NR	Y	mean: 780	NR	mean: 4.3	0/19	mean: 113	NR
	RO	19/33 (57.6)	mean: 3,672.84 p = 0.012	NR	NR		mean: 780 p=1	NR	mean: 3.5 p=0.527	1/19 (5) p=0.383	mean: 152 p=0.04	NR
Hagen, 2012 [43]	OP	524/990 (52.9)	mean: 16,851	NR	NR	NR	mean: 1,869	NR	mean (range): 10.9 (5-220)	-	NR	NR

First author, Year [ref]	Type of operation	Number of patients (%)	Total costs	Operative charges	Non-operative charges	Robot cost included (Y/N)	Surgical equipment costs	Operating room costs	Length of hospital stay (days)	Conversion to laparotomy (%)	Duration of surgery (min)	Blood loss (mL)
Roux-en-Y gastric bypass												
	LA	323/990 (32.6)	mean: 15,897	NR	NR		mean: 4,025	NR	mean (range): 11 (5-249)	16/323 (4.9)	NR	NR
	RO	143/990 (14.5)	mean: 14,187	NR	NR		mean: 3,845	NR	mean (range): 7.4 (4-24)	2/143 (1.4) p=0.038	NR	NR
Scozzari, 2011 [44]	LA	423/533 (79.4)	mean: 4,658.28	mean: 2,318.28	mean: 2,340	Y	mean: 765.78	mean: 1,402.5	mean (range): 8.3 (3-99)	0/423	mean (range): 187 (75-360)	NR
	RO	110/533 (20.6)	mean: 5,777.76 p<0.001	mean: 3287.76	mean: 2,490		mean: 1,581.51	mean: 1,856.25	mean (range): 7.8 (3-65) p=NS	0/110	mean (range): 247.5 (90-405) p<0.001	NR
Curet, 2009 [45]	LAH	36/135 (26.7)	mean: 50,408	NR	mean: 42,055	NR	NR	NR	mean: 3.3	NR	mean: 183.3	NR
	LAS	78/135 (57.8)	mean: 48,503	NR	mean: 39,418		NR	NR	mean: 3.6	NR	mean: 185.6	NR
	RO	21/135 (15.5)	mean: 57,002 p = 0.047	NR	mean: 48,796 p = 0.015		NR	NR	mean: 3 p = 0.13	NR	mean: 181.7 p = 0.92	NR
Schraibman, 2014 [46]	LA	32/48 (66.7)	mean (range): 9,972 (23,518-54,645)	mean (range): 7,138 (17,299-46,725)	NR	Y	NR	NR	median (1st-3rd quartile): 3 (2-4)	NR	median (1st-3rd quartile): 138 (115-170)	NR

Table 1. (Continued)

First author, Year [ref]	Type of operation	Number of patients (%)	Total costs	Operative charges	Non-operative charges	Robot cost included (Y/N)	Surgical equipment costs	Operating room costs	Length of hospital stay (days)	Conversion to laparotomy (%)	Duration of surgery (min)	Blood loss (mL)
Sleeve Gastrectomy												
	RO	16/48 (33.3)	mean (range): 15,521 (11,433-98,568) p < 0.001	mean (range): 13,670 (8,532-20,144) p < 0.001	NR		NR	NR	median (1st-3rd quartile): 3 (2-4) p = 0.766	NR	median (1st-3rd quartile): 148 (133-168) p = 0.211	NR
Splenectomy												
Gelmini, 2011 [47]	LA	45/90 (50)	median: 1,898	NR	NR	NR	NR	NR	median: 5.3	5/45 (11.1)	median: 125	NR
	RO	45/90 (50)	median: 5,077 p < 0.05	NR	NR		NR	NR	median: 5.1 p=NS	4/45 (8.9) p=NS	median: 153 p<0.05	NR
Bodner, 2005 [48]	LA	6/12 (50)	NR	mean: 2,992	NR	Y	NR	NR	mean (range): 6 (4-7)	0/12	mean (range): 127 (95-174)	mean: <50
	RO	6/12 (50)	NR	mean: 5,075 p < 0.05	NR		mean: 957	NR	mean (range): 7 (5-11) p < 0.05	0/12	mean (range): 154 (115-292) p < 0.05	mean: <50

Abbreviations: OP = open, LA = laparoscopic, RO = robotic, NR = not referred, NA= not applicable, Y = Yes, N =No, hr = hour, SD = standard deviation, SEM=standard error of mean, NS= not statistically significant, LAH = laparoscopic handsewn technique, LAS = laparoscopic stapled technique. †All costs are estimated in Euros. ††Expressed in hours. *Comparison between open and robotic.

** Comparison between open and laparoscopy.

*** Comparison between laparoscopy and robotics.

‡ Adjusted median.

The implement of robotic technology in operations of general surgery represent a novelty that may influence both the surgical treatment of numerous pathologies and the post operative outcomes. The robotic assisted surgery has serious possibilities to evolve in a cost-effective technique especially in centers with large number of cases, in spite of the undeniable elevated costs of acquisition and maintenance. Having as intention to increase the use of this surgical technique, it should be utilized not only on clinical treatment of patients but as well for the surgical training of all residents. The possible future industry competition in correlation with the technological development may steadily reduce the cost of the robotic equipment, making robotics a more cost-effective and affordable technique.

REFERENCES

[1] Yu, HY; Friedlander, DF; Patel, S; Hu, JC. The current status of robotic oncologic surgery. *CA Cancer J Clin.*, 2013, 63, 45-56.

[2] Boggi, U; Signori, S; De Lio, N; et al. Feasibility of robotic pancreaticoduodenectomy. *Br J Surg.*, 2013, 100, 917-25.

[3] Smith, JA; Jr. Herrell, SD. Robotic-assisted laparoscopic prostatectomy: do minimally invasive approaches offer significant advantages? *J Clin Oncol.*, 2005, 23, 8170-5.

[4] van Dam, P; Hauspy, J; Verkinderen, L; et al. Are costs of robot-assisted surgery warranted for gynecological procedures? *Obstet Gynecol Int.*, 2011, 2011, 973830.

[5] Lotan, Y. Is robotic surgery cost-effective: no. *Curr Opin Urol.*, 2012, 22, 66-9.

[6] Heemskerk, J; Bouvy, ND; Baeten, CG. The end of robot-assisted laparoscopy? A critical appraisal of scientific evidence on the use of robot-assisted laparoscopic surgery. *Surg Endosc.*, 2014, 28, 1388-98.

[7] Turchetti, G; Palla, I; Pierotti, F; Cuschieri, A. Economic evaluation of da Vinci-assisted robotic surgery: a systematic review. *Surg Endosc.*, 2012, 26, 598-606.

[8] Intuitive, Surgical. In: Wikipedia, the free encyclopedia. http:// en.wikipedia.org/ wiki/ Intuitive_Surgical Accessed on 11 Nov 2015.

[9] Steinberg, PL; Merguerian, PA; Bihrle, W; 3rd, Seigne, JD. The cost of learning robotic-assisted prostatectomy. *Urology.*, 2008, 72, 1068-72.

[10] Albani, JM; Lee, DI. Virtual reality-assisted robotic surgery simulation. *J Endourol.*, 2007, 21, 285-7.

[11] Iavazzo, C; Papadopoulou, EK; Gkegkes, ID. Cost assessment of robotics in gynecologic surgery: A systematic review. *J Obstet Gynaecol Res.*, 2014, 40, 2125-34.

[12] Blackmore, AE; Wong, MT; Tang, CL. Evolution of laparoscopy in colorectal surgery: an evidence-based review. *World J Gastroenterol.*, 2014, 20, 4926-33.

[13] Ng, AT; Tam, PC. Current status of robot-assisted surgery. *Hong Kong Med J.*, 2014, 20, 241-50.

[14] Gorter, RR; Heij, HA; Eker, HH; Kazemier, G. Laparoscopic appendectomy: State of the art. Tailored approach to the application of laparoscopic appendectomy? *Best Pract Res Clin Gastroenterol.*, 2014, 28, 211-24.

[15] Magrina, JF. Outcomes of laparoscopic treatment for endometrial cancer. *Curr Opin Obstet Gynecol.*, 2005, 17, 343-6.

[16] Schreuder, HW; Verheijen, RH. Robotic surgery. *BJOG.*, 2009, 116, 198-213.

[17] Seamon, LG; Cohn, DE; Henretta, MS; et al. Minimally invasive comprehensive surgical staging for endometrial cancer: Robotics or laparoscopy? *Gynecol Oncol.*, 2009, 113, 36-41.

[18] Salman, M; Bell, T; Martin, J; Bhuva, K; Grim, R; Ahuja, V. Use, cost, complications, and mortality of robotic versus nonrobotic general surgery procedures based on a nationwide database. *Am Surg.*, 2013, 79, 553-60.

[19] Brunaud, L; Ayav, A; Zarnegar, R; et al. Prospective evaluation of 100 robotic-assisted unilateral adrenalectomies. *Surgery.*, 2008, 144, 995-1001.

[20] Prewitt, R; Bochkarev V; McBride, CL; et al. The patterns and costs of the Da Vinci robotic surgery system in a large academic institution, *J Robotic Surg.*, 2008, 2, 17-20.

[21] Winter, JM; Talamini, MA; Stanfield, CL, et al. Thirty robotic adrenalectomies: a single institution's experience. *Surg Endosc.*, 2006, 20, 119-24.

[22] Morino, M; Beninca, G; Giraudo, G; Del Genio, GM; Rebecchi, F; Garrone, C. Robot-assisted vs laparoscopic adrenalectomy: a prospective randomized controlled trial. *Surg Endosc.*, 2004, 18, 1742-6.

[23] Muhlmann, G; Klaus, A; Kirchmayr, W; et al. DaVinci robotic-assisted laparoscopic bariatric surgery: is it justified in a routine setting? *Obes Surg.*, 2003, 13, 848-54.

[24] Buzad, FA; Corne, LM; Brown, TC; et al. Single-site robotic cholecystectomy: efficiency and cost analysis. *Int J Med Robot.*, 2013, 9, 365-70.

[25] Breitenstein, S; Nocito, A; Puhan, M; Held, U; Weber, M; Clavien, PA. Robotic-assisted versus laparoscopic cholecystectomy: outcome and cost analyses of a case-matched control study. *Ann Surg.*, 2008, 247, 987-93.

[26] Heemskerk, J; van Dam, R; van Gemert, WG; et al. First results after introduction of the four-armed da Vinci Surgical System in fully robotic laparoscopic cholecystectomy. *Dig Surg.*, 2005, 22, 426-31.

[27] Keller, DS; Senagore, AJ; Lawrence, JK; Champagne, BJ; Delaney, CP. Comparative effectiveness of laparoscopic versus robot-assisted colorectal resection. *Surg Endosc.*, 2014, 28, 212-21.

[28] Park, JS; Choi, GS; Park, SY; Kim, HJ; Ryuk, JP. Randomized clinical trial of robot-assisted versus standard laparoscopic right colectomy. *Br J Surg.*, 2012, 99, 1219-26.

[29] Bertani, E; Chiappa, A; Biffi, R; et al. Assessing appropriateness for elective colorectal cancer surgery: clinical, oncological, and quality-of-life short-term outcomes employing different treatment approaches. *Int J Colorectal Dis.*, 2011, 26, 1317-27.

[30] deSouza, AL; Prasad, LM; Park, JJ; Marecik, SJ; Blumetti, J; Abcarian, H. Robotic assistance in right hemicolectomy: is there a role? *Dis Colon Rectum.*, 2010, 53, 1000-6.

[31] Rawlings, AL; Woodland, JH; Vegunta, RK; Crawford, DL. Robotic versus laparoscopic colectomy. *Surg Endosc.*, 2007, 21, 1701-8.

[32] Baek, SJ; Kim, SH; Cho, JS; Shin, JW; Kim, J. Robotic versus conventional laparoscopic surgery for rectal cancer: a cost analysis from a single institute in Korea. *World J Surg.*, 2012, 36, 2722-9.

[33] Wormer, BA; Dacey, KT; Williams, KB; et al. The first nationwide evaluation of robotic general surgery: a regionalized, small but safe start. *Surg Endosc.*, 2014, 28, 767-76.

[34] Owen, B; Simorov, A; Siref, A; Shostrom, V; Oleynikov, D. How does robotic anti-reflux surgery compare with traditional open and laparoscopic techniques: a cost and outcomes analysis. *Surg Endosc.*, 2014, 28, 1686-90.

[35] Nakadi, IE; Melot, C; Closset, J; et al. Evaluation of da Vinci Nissen fundoplication clinical results and cost minimization. *World J Surg.*, 2006, 30, 1050-4.

[36] Anderberg, M; Kockum, CC; Arnbjornsson, E. Paediatric robotic surgery in clinical practice: a cost analysis. *Eur J Pediatr Surg.*, 2009, 19, 311-5.

[37] Heemskerk, J; van Gemert, WG; Greve, JW; Bouvy, ND. Robot-assisted versus conventional laparoscopic Nissen fundoplication: a comparative retrospective study on costs and time consumption. *Surg Laparosc Endosc Percutan Tech.*, 2007, 17, 1-4.

[38] Muller-Stich, BP; Reiter, MA; Wente, MN; et al. Robot-assisted versus conventional laparoscopic fundoplication: short-term outcome of a pilot randomized controlled trial. *Surg Endosc.*, 2007, 21, 1800-5.

[39] Morino, M; Pellegrino, L; Giaccone, C; Garrone, C; Rebecchi, F. Randomized clinical trial of robot-assisted versus laparoscopic Nissen fundoplication. *Br J Surg.*, 2006, 93, 553-8.

[40] Kang, CM; Kim, DH; Lee, WJ; Chi, HS. Conventional laparoscopic and robot-assisted spleen-preserving pancreatectomy: does da Vinci have clinical advantages? *Surg Endosc.*, 2011, 25, 2004-9.

[41] Waters, JA; Canal, DF; Wiebke, EA; et al. Robotic distal pancreatectomy: cost effective? *Surgery.*, 2010, 148, 814-23.

[42] Heemskerk, J; de Hoog, DE; van Gemert, WG; Baeten, CG; Greve, JW; Bouvy, ND. Robot-assisted vs. conventional laparoscopic rectopexy for rectal prolapse: a comparative study on costs and time. *Dis Colon Rectum.*, 2007, 50, 1825-30.

[43] Hagen, ME; Pugin, F; Chassot, G; et al. Reducing cost of surgery by avoiding complications: the model of robotic Roux-en-Y gastric bypass. *Obes Surg.*, 2012, 22, 52-61.

[44] Scozzari, G; Rebecchi, F; Millo, P; Rocchietto, S; Allieta, R; Morino, M. Robot-assisted gastrojejunal anastomosis does not improve the results of the laparoscopic Roux-en-Y gastric bypass. *Surg Endosc.*, 2011, 25, 597-603.

[45] Curet, MJ; Curet M; Solomon, H; et al. Comparison of hospital charges between robotic, laparoscopic stapled, and laparoscopic handsewn Roux-en-Y gastric bypass, *J Robotic Surg.*, 2009, 3, 75-78.

[46] Schraibman, V; Macedo, AL; Epstein, MG; et al. Comparison of the morbidity, weight loss, and relative costs between robotic and laparoscopic sleeve gastrectomy for the treatment of obesity in Brazil. *Obes Surg.*, 2014, 24, 1420-4.

[47] Gelmini, R; Franzoni, C; Spaziani, A; Patriti, A; Casciola, L; Saviano, M. Laparoscopic splenectomy: conventional versus robotic approach--a comparative study. *J Laparoendosc Adv Surg Tech A.*, 2011, 21, 393-8.

[48] Bodner, J; Kafka-Ritsch, R; Lucciarini, P; Fish, JH; 3rd, Schmid, T. A critical comparison of robotic versus conventional laparoscopic splenectomies. *World J Surg.*, 2005, 29, 982-5, discussion 5-6.

In: Health Care Costs
Editor: Brandon Hill
ISBN: 978-1-63484-619-6

Chapter 3

COST ANALYSIS OF DA VINCI® ROBOT APPLICATION IN GYNAECOLOGICAL OPERATIONS

Christos Iavazzo*[1], *MD, PhD,
and Ioannis D. Gkegkes*[2], *MD, PhD
[1]Gynaecological Oncology Department, Christie Hospital,
Manchester, United Kingdom
[2]First Department of Surgery, General Hospital of Attica "KAT,"
Athens, Greece

ABSTRACT

The application of robotics is an innovation in the field of gynecologic surgery. Specific characteristics of robotic assisted surgery, such as the 3-dimention view of the surgical field, the elimination of surgeon's natural tremor and the existence of wristed instruments, improve operator's dexterity and make easier every operation into the pelvis or retroperitoneally. On the other hand, the high cost of acquisition, maintenance and instrumentation, make the use of robotic systems an unaffordable luxury for countries of the developing world. Nevertheless, robotic surgery has the potential to become cost-effective in centers with many patients while industry competition could reduce the cost of the robotic instrumentation, making robotic technology more affordable and cost-effective.

The last decade, robotic assisted surgery has made great progress and became popular in various surgical fields such as urology, general surgery, head/neck surgery, thoracic surgery and gynaecology [1]. Smaller incisions, shorter length of hospital stay, lower intraoperative blood loss, minimal need for blood transfusion and decreased postoperative pain are some of the major advantages of robotic assisted surgery over open surgical technique [1, 2] In addition, robotic surgery, may improve the surgical time compared with laparoscopy as it allows a three dimensional view of the operating field, eliminating surgeon tremor, permits more precise movements while the use of wristed instruments improves dexterity and facilitates easier suturing into the abdominal cavity [3] On the other hand, the lack of tactile feedback and the high cost related to robotic surgery are the main disadvantages. Nevertheless, the elevated cost of acquisition as well as of maintenance of the robotic system (necessitating an annual service contract, 10% of the initial cost) represents the most important factor that causes drawback at the dissemination of robotic assisted surgery [3].

The current cost of the da Vinci® robotic equipment is relatively high and includes the acquisition, training and equipment-instrument cost. The initial capital for the acquisition of robotic devices can be amortized in a period longer of 7 years, which can be interpreted with an amount over 1,000 Euros per patient, if we considered that it is used for 300 or more procedures per year [3]. As it can be deduced, if it is used for a lower volume of patients, this would result in higher per case charges. The robotic instruments have a limited number of uses (10 lives per instrument) whereas the charges per instrument are approximately over 1,500 Euros [4]. Nevertheless, the reimbursement to the hospital for utilization of the robot depends on the type of health insurance and on the health system.

In eras of economic recession even for European Community countries such as Greece, the strength of healthcare systems is tested. With the intention to maintain the basic structure and function of a health system, the costs are usually undergoing substantial cuts. The adjustment of a healthcare system to new financial conditions necessitates also the costs analysis of the various techniques and procedures, especially in the surgical fields. Although cost studies are difficult to accomplish, it is imperative that physicians and society as a whole must understand the impact of the cost of robotics. The comparison of innovative minimally invasive methods and standard surgical techniques therefore is essential. Furthermore, the operative costs among the different surgical approaches are influenced by the necessity of specialized equipment. In particular, the robotic assisted surgery uses equipment of elevated cost in part due to the innovation of the technique and in part of the high specialization of the equipment, which could not have a multipurpose utility as for instance the instruments of the standard laparoscopy can not be used [4]. The acquisition cost of the only available system on the market is over 1 million Euros while the maintenance costs per year are almost 150,000 Euros. In order to amortize the costs of robotic equipment, the health care structures can rely on elevated number of cases being operated as Van Dam et al. has proved [3]. Moreover, the lack of market competition is one of the major factors that keep elevated the costs of robot-related instrumentation. More specifically, in the early 1980's, the first robot surgical systems were developed [5]. The application of robots on gynecologic surgery was described for first time with the use of Zeus device (Computer Motion Inc), a competitor of da Vinci® surgical system (Intuitive Surgical, CA) [6]. Computer Motion, which had been presented into the robotic surgery systems market earlier than Intuitive Surgical, sued for patent infringement Intuitive Surgical. The dispute between the two companies had as consequence, in 2003, the merge of the ultimate market domination in favor of the da Vinci® system [7].

The variation of the operating time is also an important factor that may influence the total surgical costs. The need of reduced operating time becomes more obvious in case of private health structures. Operating time charges are generally calculated in intervals of 15 to 30 minutes. During the robotic approach, the setup of the equipment is considerably longer compared to the laparoscopic or open surgery procedure but of course this can be improved when a well trained surgical team is implicated in the set up [8]. Moreover, the operative time depends on the experience of both the operator and the surgical team. The learning curve may present great variation being subject to the surgeon's capability [3]. Also, the costs related to the learning curve are considered as elevated or more often as an additional cost due to the fact that surgeons already went through a training program for open and laparoscopic operations [9]. At this point, it should be mentioned that in order to reduce the costs related to learning curve is necessary the presence of high case load as well as the need of virtual reality simulators [9, 10].

Minimal invasive surgery has been shown to have benefits over laparotomy for the treatment of patients with a variety of gynaecologic pathologies [11, 12]. Smaller incision, which diminishes both the post-operative pain and shortens recovery time, reduced hemorrhaging, better cosmetic result and less complications are some of the principal advantages of minimal invasive surgery over the open surgical method. Especially, robotic procedures can minimize the cost of operating in elderly or morbidly obese patients with comorbidities as it minimizes the hospital stay in these patients. Moreover, lack of depth perception or limited range of motion at the surgical site which were some of the major limitations of laparoscopic surgery are now overcome with the use of da Vinci® robot [13]. In the field of gynaecologic surgery, as far as the overall costs between both open and laparoscopic approach no statistically significant difference can be found [11].

The duration of hospital stay has also a substantial impact on the overall charge of hospitalization. All mini-invasive surgical techniques (both robotic and laparoscopic approach) as it is obvious have generally limited hospital stay in comparison with the open methods [4]. For this reason, the obtained cost savings due to the decreased number of hospital days can compensate the increased operative expenses of the mini-invasive techniques. For example, patients treated robotically or laparoscopically have a mean hospitalization of 1-2 days while those with open surgery for more than 4 days [14, 15]. In Tan Kim et al. study, even though the maximum hospital stay was 42 days, the median duration was 1 day [16]. Moreover, the costs of hospitalization are also in correlation with the type of health care structure, the health system and the type of health insurance [3, 17]. Cost data on this field is difficult to be analyzed as those differ between countries, private or public sectors. Different opinions are raised regarding the comparison of robotic procedures to laparoscopy, there are studies that claim that the reduced hospital stay after robotic surgery in comparison with laparoscopy may present a financial advantage over the standard laparoscopic procedures [18]. Other studies showed closely similar advantages between these two minimally invasive techniques [19]. At the moment, it seems that laparoscopy is a more economic minimal invasive method compared to robotic procedures [20, 21]. One of the main future goals is to clarify how robotic procedures could become a superior method compared to laparoscopy regarding cost.

As it was shown from our data analysis presented in Table 1 - the majority of which referred to hysterectomy - robotic is more expensive compared to laparoscopy which in turn is more expensive compared to open surgery. Although, the cost of buying the robot, professional cost, surgical equipment cost, operating room cost varies in the different studies, we believe that it could be minimized if we also analyze the minimal hospital stay, the quicker return to normal activities of the patient as well as his/her family members, the minimal conversion rates to laparotomy and the minimal blood loss. Moreover, the improvement in training of all the personnel will minimize the surgical time and so the cost analysis is definitely in favor of minimal invasive techniques.

Table 1. Costs related to equipment and peri-operative outcomes†

First author, Year [ref]	Type of operation	Number of patients (%)	Total costs	Operative charges	Non-operative charges	Robot cost included (Y/N)	Professionals' costs	Surgical equipment costs	Operating room costs	Length of hospital stay (days)	Conversion to laparotomy (%)	Duration of surgery (min)	Blood loss (mL)
Hysterectomy													
Desille-Gbaguidi, 2013 [20]	LA	endometrium cancer group: 15/57 (26)	mean (±SD): 6,666 (1,963)	mean (±SD): 2,733 (735)	mean (±SD): 4,142 (1,550)	Y	NR	mean: 91,393	43,363/hr	mean (±SD): 5.27 (2.12)	5/57 (8.7)	mean (±SD): 239 (101)	mean (±SD): 423 (312)
		cervix cancer group: 12/57 (21)	mean (±SD): 7,803 (2,130)	mean (±SD): 3,239 (542)	mean (±SD): 3,879 (1,456)		NR	mean: 91,393	43,363/hr	mean (±SD): 5.83 (1.99)		mean (±SD): 288 (79)	mean (±SD): 477 (477)
	RO	endometrium cancer group: 20/57 (35)	mean (±SD): 10,816 (1,935), p < 0.0001	mean (±SD): 7,402 (1,733), p < 0.0001	mean (±SD): 3,435 (989), p = 0.39		NR	mean: 148,308	84,921/hr	mean (±SD): 4.60 (1.35), p = 0.39	3/57 (5.3)	mean (±SD): 269 (74), p = 0.08	mean (±SD): 376 (692), p = 0.30
		cervix cancer group: 10/57 (18)	mean (±SD): 12,211 (3,252), p=0.001	mean (±SD): 8,501 (1,451), p<0.0001	mean (±SD): 3,362 (2,287), p=0.07		NR	mean: 148,308	84,921/hr	mean (±SD): 4.70 (3.13), p = 0.07		mean (±SD): 291 (84), p = 0.71	mean (±SD): 301 (236), p = 0.48
Reynisson, 2013 [22]	OP	51/231 (22.1)	mean: 9,854	NR	NR	Y	NR	NR	NR	mean: 7.3	-	mean: 233	median (range): 100 (25-1300)

Table 1. (Continued)

First author, Year [ref]	Type of operation	Number of patients (%)	Total costs	Operative charges	Non-operative charges	Robot cost included (Y/N)	Professionals' costs	Surgical equipment costs	Operating room costs	Length of hospital stay (days)	Conversion to laparotomy (%)	Duration of surgery (min)	Blood loss (mL)
	RO	180/231 (77.9)	mean range: 9,682–13,949	NR	NR		NR	NR	NR	mean range: 2.4-5.5	2/180 (1.1)	mean range: 201-314	median (range): 700 (150-2900), p < 0.0001
Coronado, 2012 [23]	OP	192/347 (55.3)	mean (±SD): 4,680.7 (1,860.3)	mean (±SD): 1,144.5 (206.3)	mean (±SD): 4,384.5 (2,932.9)	Y	NR	NR	NR	mean (±SD): 8.1 (4.8)	-	mean (±SD): 157.4 (32.9)	mean (±SD): 231.5 (109.5)
	LA	84/347 (24.2)	mean (±SD): 4,594.3 (1,447.8)	mean (±SD): 2,334.5 (334.1)	mean (±SD): 2,694.3 (2,547.5)		NR	NR	NR	mean (±SD): 4.6 (4)	7/84 (8.3)	mean (±SD): 218.2 (54.3)	mean (±SD): 190 (119.7)
	RO	71/347 (20.5)	mean (±SD): 5,043.3 (2,370.1)	mean (±SD): 3,018.4 (500.5)	mean (±SD): 2,045.2 (2019.6)		NR	NR	NR	mean (±SD): 3.5 (3.4)	3/71 (4.2)	mean (±SD): 189.2 (35.4)	mean (±SD): 99.4 (75.4)
Dennis, 2012 [24]	OP	NR	in 2006: mean: 894	NR	NR	Y	NR	NR	NR	NR	NR	NR	NR
	LA	NR	in 2006: mean: 411	NR	NR		NR	NR	NR	NR	NR	NR	NR

First author, Year [ref]	Type of operation	Number of patients (%)	Total costs	Operative charges	Non-operative charges	Robot cost included (Y/N)	Professionals' costs	Surgical equipment costs	Operating room costs	Length of hospital stay (days)	Conversion to laparotomy (%)	Duration of surgery (min)	Blood loss (mL)
	RO	in 2008: 13 in 2009: 24	in 2008: mean: 2,207 in 2009: mean: 1,731	NR	NR		NR	in 2008: mean: 1,856 in 2009: mean: 1,440	in 2008: mean: 51 in 2009: mean: 48	NR	NR	NR	NR
Lau 2012, [25]	OP	160/303 (52.8)	mean (95% CI): 7,553	NR	mean (95% CI): 4,826 (4,284-5,367)	Y	mean (95% CI): 504 (499-511)	NR	mean (95% CI): 172 (147-197)	mean (IQR): 5.5 (4-6)	-	mean (IQR): 207 (158.5-243.5)	mean (IQR): 266 (100-300)
	RO	143/303 (47.2)	mean (95% CI): 5,568, p < 0.001	NR	mean (95% CI): 2,658 (1,814-3,503), p < 0.001		mean (95% CI): 598 (598-598), p < 0.001	NR	mean (95% CI): 2,168 (2,168-2,168), p < 0.001	mean (IQR): 2.2 (1-2), p < 0.001	3/303 (4.2)	mean (IQR): 241 (205-272), p < 0.001	mean (IQR): 73 (20-100), p < 0.001
Scribner, 2012 [26]	LA	48/76 (63.2)	median (range): 17,094 (12,159-25,813)	median (range): 2,181 (12,159-25,813)	median (range): 692 (467-1,428)	Y	NR	median (range): 109 (25-220)	median (range): 1,052 (353-1,443)	1	0/48	mean (range): 124 (74-201)	mean (range): 83.9 (25-450)

Table 1. (Continued)

First author, Year [ref]	Type of operation	Number of patients (%)	Total costs	Operative charges	Non-operative charges	Robot cost included (Y/N)	Professionals' costs	Surgical equipment costs	Operating room costs	Length of hospital stay (days)	Conversion to laparotomy (%)	Duration of surgery (min)	Blood loss (mL)
	RO	28/76 (36.8)	median (range): 23,316 (16,988-41,182), p < 0.001	median (range): 3,617 (2,477-9,085), p < 0.001	median (range): 692 (492-3,389), p = 0.4		NR	median (range): 145 (48-220), p=0.001	median (range): 2,001 (950-6,181), p<0.001	1.3, p=0.005	0/28	mean (range): 170 (68-260), p<0.001	mean (range): 104.4 (25-250), p=0.3
Venkat, 2012 [27]	LA	27/54 (50)	mean: 41,[illegible]36	NR	NR	NR	mean: 4,801	NR	mean: 18,886	mean: 1.8	NR	mean: 184	mean: 316.7
	RO	27/54 (50)	mean: 48,769, p = 0.0[illegible]	NR	NR		mean: 5,178, p = 0.033	NR	mean: 24,891, p < 0.001	mean: 1.7, p = 0.63	NR	mean: 265, p < 0.001	mean: 220.4, p = 0.13
Wright, 2012 [28]	OP	1610/1894 (85)	median: 7,298	NR	NR	NR	NR	NR	NR	median (IQR): 3 (3-4)	-	NR	NR
	LA	217/1894 (11.5)	median: 8,934	NR	NR		NR	NR	NR	median (IQR): 2 (1-2)	NR	NR	NR
	RO	67/1894 (3.5)	median: 7,722, p < 0.0001	NR	NR		NR	NR	NR	median (IQR): 1 (1-2), p < 0.0001	NR	NR	NR

First author, Year [ref]	**Type of operation**	**Number of patients (%)**	**Total costs**	**Operative charges**	**Non-operative charges**	**Robot cost included (Y/N)**	**Professionals' costs**	**Surgical equipment costs**	**Operating room costs**	**Length of hospital stay (days)**	**Conversion to laparotomy (%)**	**Duration of surgery (min)**	**Blood loss (mL)**
Jonsdottir, 2011 [14]	OP	in 2006: 682/1,054 (64.7) in 2009: 386/1,079 (35.7)	in 2006: mean (±SD): 10,128 (7,478) in 2009: mean (±SD): 9,621 (5,669), p < 0.147	in 2006: mean (±SD): 3,783 (1,486) in 2009: mean (±SD): 4,715 (1,540), p < 0.001	NR	Y	NR	NR	NR	in 2006: mean (±SD): 4.1 (3.4) in 2009: mean (±SD): 3.5 (2.3), p < 0.05	-	in 2006: mean (±SD): 189 (70) in 2009: mean (±SD): 196 (53)	in 2006: mean (±SD): 387 (565) in 2009: mean (±SD): 363 (388)
	LA	in 2006: 187/1,054 (17.7) in 2009: 496/1,079 (46)	in 2006: mean (±SD): 7,048 (3,073) in 2009: mean (±SD): 9,356 (4,793), p < 0.001	in 2006: mean (±SD): 4,396 (1,695) in 2009: mean (±SD): 5,850 (1,491), p < 0.001	NR		NR	NR	NR	in 2006: mean (±SD): 1.3 (1.5) in 2009: mean (±SD): 1.3 (0.9)	in 2006: 28/187 (15) in 2009: 22/496 (4.4), p < 0.0001	in 2006: mean (±SD): 210 (70) in 2009: mean (±SD): 189 (64), p < 0.001	in 2006: mean (±SD): 217 (232) in 2009: mean (±SD): 110 (144), p < 0.0001
	RO	in 2006: 22/1,054 (2) in 2009: 63/1,079 (5.8)	in 2006: mean (±SD): 12,145 (1,819) in 2009: mean (±SD): 11,004 (3,193), p < 0.001	in 2006: mean (±SD): 8,593 (1,302) in 2009: mean (±SD): 7,989 (2,252), p < 0.084	NR		NR	NR	NR	in 2006: mean (±SD): 1.2 (0.7) in 2009: mean (±SD): 1.4 (0.9)	in 2006: 3/22 (13.6) in 2009: 0/63, p<0.05	in 2006: mean (±SD): 278 (74) in 2009: mean (±SD): 260 (74)	in 2006: mean (±SD): 92 (99) in 2009: mean (±SD): 75 (162)

Table 1. (Continued)

First author, Year [ref]	Type of operation	Number of patients (%)	Total costs	Operative charges	Non-operative charges	Robot cost included (Y/N)	Professionals' costs	Surgical equipment costs	Operating room costs	Length of hospital stay (days)	Conversion to laparotomy (%)	Duration of surgery (min)	Blood loss (mL)
	VA	in 2006: 163/1,054 (15.5) in 2009: 134/1,079 (12.4)	in 2006: mean (±SD): 5,838 (1,804) in 2009: mean (±SD): 8,969 (4,553), $p <$ 0.001	in 2006: mean (±SD): 3,002 (931) in 2009: mean (±SD): 3,194 (947), $p < 0.002$	NR		NR	NR	NR	in 2006: mean (±SD): 1.7 (0.8) in 2009: mean (±SD): 1.4 (0.83), $p < 0.001$	in 2006: 1/163 (0.6) in 2009: 2/134 (1.5)	in 2006: mean (±SD): 164 (60) in 2009: mean (±SD): 153 (61)	in 2006: mean (±SD): 223 (277.9) in 2009: mean (±SD): 143 (189), $p < 0.05$
Landeen, 2011 [29]	OP	274/1474 (18.6)	mean (±SD): 5,315 (2,855), $p <$ 0.0001	mean (±SD): 3,054 (1,708), $p <$ 0.0001	mean (±SD): 2,260 (1,187), $p < 0.0001$	Y	NR	mean (±SD): 118 (150), $p <$ 0.0001	NR	mean (±SD): 2.7 (1.4), $p <$ 0.0001	-	mean (±SD): 83.7 (33.8), $p < 0.0001$	mean (±SD): 269.8 (385.3), $p <$ 0.0001
	LA	230/1474 (15.6)	mean (±SD): 5,236 (2,309), $p <$ 0.0001	mean (±SD): 3,395 (1,435), $p<0.0001$	mean (±SD): 1,840 (919), $p <$ 0.0001		NR	mean (±SD): 675 (336), $p <$ 0.0001	NR	mean (±SD): 1.8 (1.5), $p <$ 0.0001	9/230 (3.9), $p=0.013$	mean (±SD): 118.3 (45.9), $p =$ 0.948	mean (±SD): 182 (185), $p < 0.0001$
	RO	569/1474 (38.6)	mean (±SD): 6,173 (1,347)	mean (±SD): 4,651 (1,042)	mean (±SD): 1,522 (437)		NR	mean (±SD): 1,409 (412)	NR	mean (±SD): 1.3 (0.6)	5/569 (0.9)	mean (±SD): 117.2 (59.4)	mean (±SD): 109.3 (143.5)

First author, Year [ref]	Type of operation	Number of patients (%)	Total costs	Operative charges	Non-operative charges	Robot cost included (Y/N)	Professionals' costs	Surgical equipment costs	Operating room costs	Length of hospital stay (days)	Conversion to laparotomy (%)	Duration of surgery (min)	Blood loss (mL)
	VA	401/1474 (27.2)	mean (±SD): 4,177 (1,256), p < 0.0001	mean (±SD): 2,511 (871), p < 0.0001	mean (±SD): 1,666 (467), p<0.0001		NR	mean (±SD): 214 (325), p < 0.0001	NR	mean (±SD): 1.9 (0.8), p < 0.0001	4/401 (1), p=1	mean (±SD): 99.2 (45.2), p < 0.0001	mean (±SD): 190 (181.3), p < 0.0001
Shah, 2011 [30]	OP	73/234 (31.2)	NR	mean: 25,616	mean: 41,062, p < 0.01	Y	NR	NR	NR	mean: 3.84	-	mean: 192.28	mean: 255.94
		LA	118/234 (50.4)	NR	mean: 25,578		NR	NR	NR	mean: 1.44, p<0.001	6/118 (5.1)	mean: 186.8, p<0.001	mean: 105.23, p < 0.001
		RO	43/234 (18.4)	NR	mean: 33,920, p < 0.01		NR	NR	NR	mean: 1.3, p<0.001	0/43	mean: 252.6, p<0.001	mean: 41.22, p<0.001
Holtz, 2010 [31]	LA	20/33 (60.6)	median: 2,743	median: 1,555	NR	Y	NR	median: 527	median: 1,013	mean (±SD): 1.7 (1.2)	2/20 (10)	mean (±SD): 156.2 (49)	mean (±SD): 150 (111)
	RO	13/33 (39.4)	median: 3,858	median: 2,521	NR		NR	median: 1,197	median: 1,175	mean (±SD): 1.7 (0.6)	0/13	mean (±SD): 192.5 (38)	mean (±SD): 84.6 (32)

Table 1. (Continued)

First author, Year [ref]	Type of operation	Number of patients (%)	Total costs	Operative charges	Non-operative charges	Robot cost included (Y/N)	Professionals' costs	Surgical equipment costs	Operating room costs	Length of hospital stay (days)	Conversion to laparotomy (%)	Duration of surgery (min)	Blood loss (mL)
Pasic, 2010 [32]	LA	Inpatient 25,789/36,188 (71) Outpatient 8,738/36,188 (24)	mean (±SD): Inpatient§ 5,291 (885) Outpatient§§ 4,514 (616)	NR	NR	NR	NR	NR	NR	mean (±SD): Inpatient§ 1.49 (0.2) Outpatient§§ -	NR	mean (±SD): Inpatient§ 2.82 (0.46)†† Outpatient§§ 2.46 (0.4)††	NR
	RO	Inpatient 1,282/36,188 (4) Outpatient 379/36,188 (1)	mean (±SD): Inpatient§ 7,315 (1,224), p<0.01 Outpatient§§ 6,010 (821), $p < 0.01$	NR	NR		NR	NR	NR	mean (±SD): Inpatient§ 1.37 (0.18), $p < 0.01$ Outpatient§§ -	NR	mean (±SD): Inpatient§ 3.22 (0.52)††, p<0.01 Outpatient§§ 2.99 (0.48)††, $p < 0.01$	NR
Sarlos 2010 [33]	LA	40/80 (50)	mean : 2,15[illegible]	NR	NR	Y	mean (range): 1,329 (1,160-1,707)	mean: 821	NR	mean (range): 3.9 (2-7)	-	mean (range): 82.9 (55-165)	mean: <50
	RO	40/80 (50)	mean : 4,06[illegible], $p < 0.05$	NR	NR		mean (range): 1,770 (1,194-2,288), $p > 0.05$	mean : 2,296	NR	mean (range): 3.3 (2-6), $p = 0.924$	0/40	mean (range): 108.9 (50-180), $p < 0.001$	mean (range): 81 (20-200)

First author, Year [ref]	Type of operation	Number of patients (%)	Total costs	Operative charges	Non-operative charges	Robot cost included (Y/N)	Professionals' costs	Surgical equipment costs	Operating room costs	Length of hospital stay (days)	Conversion to laparotomy (%)	Duration of surgery (min)	Blood loss (mL)
Bell, 2008 [34]	OP	40/110 (36.4)	mean: 9,822	mean (±SD): 684 (215)	mean (±SD): 4,204 (1,964)	NR	NR	mean (±SD): 684 (215)	NR	mean (±SD): 4 (1.5)	-	mean (±SD): 108.6 (41.4)	mean (±SD): 316.8 (282.1)
	LA	30/110 (27.2)	mean: 5,744	mean (±SD): 858 (139)	mean (±SD): 1,522 (188)		NR	mean (±SD): 858 (138)	NR	mean (±SD): 2 (1.2)	NR	mean (±SD): 171.1 (36.2)	mean (±SD): 253 (427.7)
	RO	40/110 (36.4)	mean: 6,231	mean (±SD): 936 (157)	mean (±SD): 1,677 (316)		NR	mean (±SD): 936 (157)	NR	mean (±SD): 2.3 (1.3)	NR	mean (±SD): 184 (41.3)	mean (±SD): 166 (225.9)
Myomectomy													
Nash, 2012 [35]	OP	106/133 (79.7)	mean (±SD): 20,277 (5,941)	NR	NR	NR	NR	NR	mean (±SD): 12,928 (3,427)	mean (±SD): 2.3 (0.66)	-	mean (±SD): 114.54 (39.06)	median: 150
	RO	27/133 (20.3)	mean (±SD): 36,029 (8,258), P < 0.0001	NR	NR		NR	NR	mean (±SD): 28,762 (7,834), p<0.0001	mean (±SD): 0.7 (0.91), p = 0.001	NR	mean (±SD): 226.41 (88.33), p < 0.0001	median: 150, p=0.2
Nezhat, 2009 [15]	LA	35/50 (70)	mean: 26,181	NR	NR	Y	NR	NR	NR	mean (range): 1.05 (1-3)	0/35	mean (range): 203 (95-330)	mean (range): 420 (110-750)

Table 1. (Continued)

First author, Year [ref]	Type of operation	Number of patients (%)	Total costs	Operative charges	Non-operative charges	Robot cost included (Y/N)	Professionals' costs	Surgical equipment costs	Operating room costs	Length of hospital stay (days)	Conversion to laparotomy (%)	Duration of surgery (min)	Blood loss (mL)
	RO	15/50 (30)	mean: 42,497	NR	NR		NR	NR	NR	mean (range): 1 (1-1), p=0.12	0/15	mean (range): 234 (140-445), p=0.03	mean (range): 370 (150-500), p=2
Advincula, 2007 [36]	OP	29/58 (50)	mean (±SD): 13,709 (6,075)	NR	NR	Y	mean (±SD): 3,539 (487)	NR	NR	mean (±SD): 3.62 (1.50)	-	mean (±SD): 154.41 (43.14)	mean (±SD): 364.66 (473.28)
	RO	29/58 (50)	mean (±SD): 27,342 (5,270), p < 0.0001	NR	NR		mean (±SD): 4,512 (1,098), p = 0.0002	NR	NR	mean (±SD): 1.48 (0.95), p < 0.0001	2/29 (6.9)	mean (±SD): 231.38 (85.10), p < 0.0001	mean (±SD): 195.69 (228.55), p = 0.0112
Sacrocolpopexy													
Elliott, 2012 [37]	OP	19/59 (32.2)	mean: 8,580	NR	NR	NR	NR	NR	NR	mean (range): 3.3 (1-11)	NR	mean (range): 221 (101-401)	mean (range): 224 (75-400)
	RO	40/59 (67.8)	mean: 7,723	NR	NR		NR	NR	NR	mean (range): 1 (0-2), p < 0.001	NR	mean (range): 226 (150-439), p = 0.725	mean (range): 63 (25-250), p < 0.001

First author, Year [ref]	Type of operation	Number of patients (%)	Total costs	Operative charges	Non-operative charges	Robot cost included (Y/N)	Professionals' costs	Surgical equipment costs	Operating room costs	Length of hospital stay (days)	Conversion to laparotomy (%)	Duration of surgery (min)	Blood loss (mL)
Hoyte, 2012 [38]	OP	91/164 (55.5)	median (range): 8,160 (5,045-88,984)	median (range): 5,701 (2,904-69,792)	median (range): 2,473 (1,617-19,190)	Y	NR	median (range): 2,286 (273-5,036)	median (range): 1,001 (639-2,863)	median (range): 3 (1-25)	-	median (range): 166 (99-394)	median (range): 150 (25-700)
	RO	73/164 (44.5)	median: 5,060 (2,772-6,798), $p < 0.001$	median (range): 5,038 (3,249-7,275), $p = 0.001$	median (range): 2,381 (651-3,546), $p = 0.043$		NR	median (range): 1,410 (138-3,014), $p = 0.002$	median (range): 1,555 (909-2,171), $p < 0.001$	median (range): 2 (1-5), $p < 0.001$	NR	median (range): 212 (119-380), $p < 0.001$	median (range): 50 (20-250), $p < 0.001$
Paraiso, 2011 [39]	LA	38/78 (48.7)	mean (±SD): 10,883 (2,231)	NR	NR	NR	NR	NR	NR	mean (±SD): 34 (11)[††]	NR	mean (±SD): 199 (46)	NR
	RO	40/78 (51.3)	mean (±SD): 12,352 (2,524)	NR	NR		NR	NR	NR	mean (±SD): 43 (37)[††], $p=0.17$	NR	mean (±SD): 265 (50), $p<0.001$	NR
Tan Kim, 2011 [16]	LA	61/104 (58.7)	NR	mean (±SD): 1,741 (259)[‡]	mean (±SD): 341 (90)[‡]	NR	NR	NR	NR	mean (range): 1 (0-42)	NR	mean (±SD): 206 (42)	mean (±SD): 85 (46)

Table 1. (Continued)

First author, Year [ref]	Type of operation	Number of patients (%)	Total costs	Operative charges	Non-operative charges	Robot cost included (Y/N)	Professionals' costs	Surgical equipment costs	Operating room costs	Length of hospital stay (days)	Conversion to laparotomy (%)	Duration of surgery (min)	Blood loss (mL)
	RO	43/104 (41.3)	NR	mean (±SD): 2,067 (313)‡, $p < 0.01$	mean (±SD): 331 (66)‡, $p = 0.738$		NR	NR	NR	mean (range): 1 (1-3), $p = 0.48$	NR	mean (±SD): 281 (58), $p < 0.001$	mean (±SD): 86 (42), $p = 0.85$
Tubal anastomosis													
Patel, 2008 [24]	OP	10/28 (35.7)	mean: 8,911	NR	NR	Y	NR	NR	NR	mean: 34.7††	NR	mean (range): 155.3 (120-183)	NR
	RO	18/28 (64.3)	mean: 10,452	NR	NR		NR	NR	NR	mean: 4††, $p = 0.0001$	NR	mean (range): 201 (140-263), $p = 0.001$	NR
Rodgers, 2007 [41]	OP	41/67 (61.2)	1,446 greater for robotic; 95%CI (843-1,375), $p < 0.001$	NR	NR	Y	NR	NR	NR	median (IQR): 142 (82-349)#	-	median (IQR): 181 (154-202)	<100: 31/67 (46.3)
	RO	26/67 (38.8)		NR	NR		NR	NR	NR	median (IQR): 99 (72-159)#, $p = 0.14$	0/67	median (IQR): 229 (205-252), $p = 0.001$	<100: 19/67 (28.4), $p = 0.48$

Abbreviations: OP = open, LA = laparoscopic, RO = robotic, VA = vaginal, NR = not referred, Y = Yes, N = No, hr = hour, IQR= interquartile range, CI = confidence interval, hr = hour. § Adjusted for the following: type of hysterectomy; robot versus non-robot; age; race; insurance type; marital status; year; indication for surgery; complex surgery; comorbid condition; census region; surgical specialty; location; hospital type; bed count; and APR-DRG severity index. §§ Adjusted for the following: type of hysterectomy; robot vs. non-robot; age; race; insurance type; marital status; year; indication for surgery; complex surgery; comorbid condition; census region; surgical specialty; location; hospital type; and bed count. ‡ Displayed in cost units. † All costs are estimated in Euros. †† Expressed in hours. # Expressed in minutes.

In the future, the extensive utilization of robotics could be established as a tool of common use in everyday surgical approach. In order to achieve this, the operative costs and the unnecessary charges should be reduced. It is fundamental for the future to create specialized robotic units operating on large number of patients per year, to minimize the number of instruments used per operation (with a maximum of 4 instead of 5), to decrease the operating time per procedure (by improving training dedicated robotic surgeons) and to opt for the early discharge of the patients when that is possible. Furthermore, it is essential the creation of competition on the market in order to reduce the price of robotic system and equipment that would make robotic assisted surgery more accessible. Another suggestion to reduce the cost is the multi-use of the robot by multi-specialties, good research of the market area covered, good training of all the team implicated, and – following examples from United Kingdom– the system could be bought by charities or research funding.

The application of robotics in the field of gynaecological surgery is an innovation which had an important impact on the surgical treatment of several pathologies. Nonetheless of the elevated costs of the acquisition and maintenance of the robotic equipment, the robotic assessed surgery has the potential to become cost-effective in case of centers with large number of patients. In order to maximize the utilization of this surgical modality should be applied not only on clinical cases but also for resident surgical training. The technological advancement and above all the industry competition could reduce the cost of the robotic instrumentation, making more affordable and cost-effective the robotic technology.

REFERENCES

[1] Yu, HY; Friedlander, DF; Patel, S; Hu, JC. The current status of robotic oncologic surgery. *CA Cancer J Clin.*, 2013, 63, 45-56.

[2] Smith, JA; Jr. Herrell, SD. Robotic-assisted laparoscopic prostatectomy: do minimally invasive approaches offer significant advantages? *J Clin Oncol.*, 2005, 23, 8170-5.

[3] van Dam, P; Hauspy, J; Verkinderen, L; et al. Are costs of robot-assisted surgery warranted for gynecological procedures? *Obstet Gynecol Int.*, 2011, 2011, 973830.

[4] Lotan, Y. Is robotic surgery cost-effective: no. *Curr Opin Urol.*, 2012, 22, 66-9.

[5] Falcone, T; Goldberg, JM; Margossian, H; Stevens, L. Robotic-assisted laparoscopic microsurgical tubal anastomosis: a human pilot study. *Fertil Steril.*, 2000, 73, 1040-2.

[6] Chen, CC; Falcone, T. Robotic gynecologic surgery: past, present, and future. *Clin Obstet Gynecol.*, 2009, 52, 335-43.

[7] Intuitive, Surgical. In: Wikipedia, the free encyclopedia. http:// en. wikipedia.org/wiki/Intuitive_Surgical Accessed 11 Nov 2015.

[8] Holloway, RW; Patel, SD; Ahmad, S. Robotic surgery in gynecology. *Scand J Surg.*, 2009, 98, 96-109.

[9] Steinberg, PL; Merguerian, PA; Bihrle, W; 3rd, Seigne, JD. The cost of learning robotic-assisted prostatectomy. *Urology.*, 2008, 72, 1068-72.

[10] Albani, JM; Lee, DI. Virtual reality-assisted robotic surgery simulation. *J Endourol.*, 2007, 21, 285-7.

[11] Magrina, JF. Outcomes of laparoscopic treatment for endometrial cancer. *Curr Opin Obstet Gynecol.*, 2005, 17, 343-6.

[12] Walsh, CA; Walsh, SR; Tang, TY; Slack, M. Total abdominal hysterectomy versus total laparoscopic hysterectomy for benign disease: a meta-analysis. *Eur J Obstet Gynecol Reprod Biol.*, 2009, 144, 3-7.

[13] Westebring-van der Putten, EP; Goossens, RH; Jakimowicz, JJ; Dankelman, J. Haptics in minimally invasive surgery--a review. *Minim Invasive Ther Allied Technol.*, 2008, 17, 3-16.

[14] Jonsdottir, GM; Jorgensen, S; Cohen, SL; et al. Increasing minimally invasive hysterectomy: effect on cost and complications. *Obstet Gynecol.*, 2011, 117, 1142-9.

[15] Nezhat, C; Lavie, O; Hsu, S; Watson, J; Barnett, O; Lemyre, M. Robotic-assisted laparoscopic myomectomy compared with standard laparoscopic myomectomy--a retrospective matched control study. *Fertil Steril.*, 2009, 91, 556-9.

[16] Tan-Kim, J; Menefee, SA; Luber, KM; Nager, CW; Lukacz, ES. Robotic assisted and laparoscopic sacrocolpopexy: comparing operative times, costs and outcomes. *Female Pelvic Med Reconstr Surg.*, 2011, 17, 44-9.

[17] Schreuder, HW; Verheijen, RH. Robotic surgery. *BJOG*, 2009, 116, 198-213.

[18] Seamon, LG; Cohn, DE; Henretta, MS; et al. Minimally invasive comprehensive surgical staging for endometrial cancer: Robotics or laparoscopy? *Gynecol Oncol.*, 2009, 113, 36-41.

[19] Pundir, J; Pundir, V; Walavalkar, R; Omanwa, K; Lancaster, G; Kayani, S. Robotic-assisted laparoscopic vs abdominal and laparoscopic

myomectomy: systematic review and meta-analysis. *J Minim Invasive Gynecol.*, 2013, 20, 335-45.

[20] Desille-Gbaguidi, H; Hebert, T; Paternotte-Villemagne, J; Gaborit, C; Rush, E; Body, G. Overall care cost comparison between robotic and laparoscopic surgery for endometrial and cervical cancer. *Eur J Obstet Gynecol Reprod Biol.*, 2013, 171(2), 348-52

[21] Barnett, JC; Judd, JP; Wu, JM; Scales, CD; Jr. Myers, ER; Havrilesky, LJ. Cost comparison among robotic, laparoscopic, and open hysterectomy for endometrial cancer. *Obstet Gynecol.*, 2010, 116, 685-93.

[22] Reynisson, P; Persson, J. Hospital costs for robot-assisted laparoscopic radical hysterectomy and pelvic lymphadenectomy. *Gynecol Oncol.*, 2013, 130, 95-9.

[23] Coronado, PJ; Herraiz, MA; Magrina, JF; Fasero, M; Vidart, JA. Comparison of perioperative outcomes and cost of robotic-assisted laparoscopy, laparoscopy and laparotomy for endometrial cancer. *Eur J Obstet Gynecol Reprod Biol.*, 2012, 165, 289-94.

[24] Dennis, T; de Mendonca, C; Phalippou, J; et al. [Study of surplus cost of robotic assistance for radical hysterectomy, versus laparotomy and standard laparoscopy]. *Gynecol Obstet Fertil.*, 2012, 40, 77-83.

[25] Lau, S; Vaknin, Z; Ramana-Kumar, AV; Halliday, D; Franco, EL; Gotlieb, WH. Outcomes and cost comparisons after introducing a robotics program for endometrial cancer surgery. *Obstet Gynecol.*, 2012, 119, 717-24.

[26] Scribner, DR; Tabitha, A; Lara-Torre, E; Weiss, PM. Cost analysis of robotic versus standard laparoscopic hysterectomies: a preliminary analysis. *J Gynecol Surg.*, 2012, 28, 255-61.

[27] Venkat, P; Chen, LM; Young-Lin, N; et al. An economic analysis of robotic versus laparoscopic surgery for endometrial cancer: costs, charges and reimbursements to hospitals and professionals. *Gynecol Oncol.*, 2012, 125, 237-40.

[28] Wright, JD; Herzog, TJ; Neugut, AI; et al. Comparative effectiveness of minimally invasive and abdominal radical hysterectomy for cervical cancer. *Gynecol Oncol.*, 2012, 127, 11-7.

[29] Landeen, LB; Bell, MC; Hubert, HB; Bennis, LY; Knutsen-Larson, SS; Seshadri-Kreaden, U. Clinical and cost comparisons for hysterectomy via abdominal, standard laparoscopic, vaginal and robot-assisted approaches. *S D Med.*, 2011, 64, 197-9, 201, 3 passim.

[30] Shah, NT; Wright, KN; Jonsdottir, GM; Jorgensen, S; Einarsson, JI; Muto, MG. The Feasibility of Societal Cost Equivalence between Robotic Hysterectomy and Alternate Hysterectomy Methods for Endometrial Cancer. *Obstet Gynecol Int.*, 2011, 2011, 570464.

[31] Holtz, DO; Miroshnichenko, G; Finnegan, MO; Chernick, M; Dunton, CJ. Endometrial cancer surgery costs: robot vs laparoscopy. *J Minim Invasive Gynecol.*, 2010, 17, 500-3.

[32] Pasic, RP; Rizzo, JA; Fang, H; Ross, S; Moore, M; Gunnarsson, C. Comparing robot-assisted with conventional laparoscopic hysterectomy: impact on cost and clinical outcomes. *J Minim Invasive Gynecol.*, 2010, 17, 730-8.

[33] Sarlos, D; Kots, L; Stevanovic, N; Schaer, G. Robotic hysterectomy versus conventional laparoscopic hysterectomy: outcome and cost analyses of a matched case-control study. *Eur J Obstet Gynecol Reprod Biol.*, 2010, 150, 92-6.

[34] Bell, MC; Torgerson, J; Seshadri-Kreaden, U; Suttle, AW; Hunt, S. Comparison of outcomes and cost for endometrial cancer staging via traditional laparotomy, standard laparoscopy and robotic techniques. *Gynecol Oncol.*, 2008, 111, 407-11.

[35] Nash, K; Feinglass, J; Zei, C; et al. Robotic-assisted laparoscopic myomectomy versus abdominal myomectomy: a comparative analysis of surgical outcomes and costs. *Arch Gynecol Obstet.*, 2012, 285, 435-40.

[36] Advincula, AP; Xu, X; Goudeau, St; Ransom, SB. Robot-assisted laparoscopic myomectomy versus abdominal myomectomy: a comparison of short-term surgical outcomes and immediate costs. *J Minim Invasive Gynecol.*, 2007, 14, 698-705.

[37] Elliott, CS; Hsieh, MH; Sokol, ER; Comiter, CV; Payne, CK; Chen, B. Robot-assisted versus open sacrocolpopexy: a cost-minimization analysis. *J Urol.*, 2012, 187, 638-43.

[38] Hoyte, L; Rabbanifard, R; Mezzich, J; Bassaly, R; Downes, K. Cost analysis of open versus robotic-assisted sacrocolpopexy. *Female Pelvic Med Reconstr Surg.*, 2012, 18, 335-9.

[39] Paraiso, MF; Jelovsek, JE; Frick, A; Chen, CC; Barber, MD. Laparoscopic compared with robotic sacrocolpopexy for vaginal prolapse: a randomized controlled trial. *Obstet Gynecol.*, 2011, 118, 1005-13.

[40] Dharia Patel, SP; Steinkampf, MP; Whitten, SJ; Malizia, BA. Robotic tubal anastomosis: surgical technique and cost effectiveness. *Fertil Steril.*, 2008, 90, 1175-9.

[41] Rodgers, AK; Goldberg, JM; Hammel, JP; Falcone, T. Tubal anastomosis by robotic compared with outpatient minilaparotomy. *Obstet Gynecol.*, 2007, 109, 1375-80.

BIBLIOGRAPHY

Access to medicines and vaccines in the South: coherence of rules and policies applied by the European Union Commission LCCN: 2011531200 Personal name: Kingah, Stephen. Main title: Access to medicines and vaccines in the South: coherence of rules and policies applied by the European Union Commission / Stephen Kingah. Published/Created: Brussel: VUB-Press, c2011. Description: 282 p.; 24 cm. Links: Publisher description http://www.loc.gov/catdir/enhancements/fy1408/2011531200-d.html Contributor biographical information http://www.loc.gov/catdir/enhancements/fy1408/2011531200-b.html ISBN: 9789054879763 9054879769 LC classification: RA401.A1 K56 2011 Related names: Vrije Universiteit Brussel. Institute for European Studies. Summary: How can developing countries maximize some of the beneficial rules and policies provided to them by the EU and international organizations to reduce public health plight in terms of inadequate access to medicines and vaccines? By navigating some of the complex European and international rules and policies that have hitherto been put in place to ease access to affordable healthcare, the author identifies ways in which policy makers and legislators can optimally use extant rules to enhance healthcare provision. Subjects: Drug accessibility--Developing countries. Pharmaceutical policy--European Union countries. Medical care, Cost of--Developing countries. Public health--Developing countries. Developing Countries. Health

Services Accessibility. Health Care Costs. Health Policy. International Cooperation--legislation & jurisprudence. Vaccines. Notes: "Based on the author's PhD thesis defended at the Faculty of Law and Criminology of the Vrije Universiteit Brussel in 2008."--Page 13. Includes bibliographical references (p. 229-259). Series: Institute for European Studies publication series; nr. 20 Publication series (Vrije Universiteit Brussel. Institute for European Studies); no. 20.

Aging in America LCCN: 2015301649 Main title: Aging in America / edited by Robert L. Scardamalia. Published/Created: Lanham, Md.: Bernan Press, c2014. Description: xxx, 416 p.: ill., maps; 29 cm. ISBN: 9781598887020 1598887025 LC classification: HQ1064.U5 A63399 2014 Related names: Scardamalia, Robert. Summary: The Baby Boom generation has breached the beginning age of retirement at 65. Today, concerns about the financial stability of Social Security, trends in disability, health care costs, and the supply of caregivers are all driven by the coming explosion in population over the age of 65. The Decennial Census and annual American Community Survey form the basis for this aging portrait. These are critical data sources because they are the only sources that provide comparable and comprehensive statistics for all communities across the nation. Many other survey sources exist that add health care and wellness indicators, but they do not provide the geographic detail coming from the Census Bureau. Aging in America contains information by state, metro area, county, city and congressional district for areas with a population of 65,000 or more.--Publisher description. Contents: Understanding the American Community Survey -- Using the ACS -- Accessing ACS data online -- More ACS resources -- Population summary -- Age structure -- Race and ethnicity -- Household relationship -- Education and language spoken at home -- Employment and labor force status -- Income and poverty -- Disability status and type -- Health insurance -- Housing summary. Subjects: Older people--United States--Statistics. Aging--Social aspects--United States. Aging--Economic aspects--United States. Aging Aged Geriatrics United States Form/Genre:

Statistics Notes: Statistical data based on the 2010 Decennial Census and the American Community Survey 2010-2012. Includes bibliographical references and index. Series: County and city extra series

Aging: concepts and controversies LCCN: 2013046946 Personal name: Moody, Harry R. Main title: Aging: concepts and controversies / Harry R. Moody, Director of Academic Affairs, AARP, Retired, Jennifer R. Sasser, Marylhurst University. Edition: 8th Edition. Published/Produced: Los Angeles: SAGE, [2015] ©2015 Description: xxxiii, 565 pages: color illustrations; 23 cm ISBN: 9781452275888 (pbk.) LC classification: HQ1064.U5 M665 2015 Related names: Sasser, Jennifer R. Contents: Preface -- Prologue -- About the authors -- Basic concepts i. a life course perspective on aging -- Urban legends of aging: “respect for elders was higher in the past” -- Suggested readings -- Urban legends of aging: “religion is good for your health” -- Focus on the future: conscious aging -- Questions for writing, reflection, and debate -- Global perspective: blue zones for longer life -- Focus on the future: “I dated a cyborg!” -- Focus on the future: late-life learning in the information society -- Basic concepts II. Aging, health care, and society -- Urban legends of aging: health care costs are high because we spend most -- Of the money on old people in the last year of life -- Focus on the future: scenarios for rationing: fiction or forecast -- Urban legends of aging: only 4% of older people live in nursing homes -- Focus on practice: long-term-care insurance -- Focus on the future: genetic screening for Alzheimer’s disease -- Urban legends of aging: older people are more likely to be victims of crime -- Focus on practice: inheritance in an aging society -- Urban legends of aging: advance directives would have prevented the -- Tragic case of Terri Schiavo -- Urban legends of aging: the gray lobby has a stranglehold on aging -- Policy in the united states -- Focus on practice: intergenerational programs -- Urban legends of aging: social security is going broke: within a few -- Decades, there won't be any money to pay promised benefits -- Focus on practice: investment decisions for retirement income -- Epilogue: finding your place in an aging society -- Appendix. how to research a term paper in gerontology -- Glossary -- Bibliography 491 -- Photo credits 519 -- Index. Subjects: Gerontology--United States. Aging--United States.

American insecurity: why our economic fears lead to political inaction LCCN: 2014023570 Personal name: Levine, Adam Seth, 1981- Main title: American insecurity: why our economic fears lead to political inaction / Adam Seth Levine. Published/Produced: Princeton: Princeton University Press, [2015] Description: xi, 302 pages: illustrations; 25 cm ISBN: 9780691162966 (hardcover: acid-free paper) LC classification: HC106.83 .L49 2015 Summary: “Americans today face no shortage of threats to their financial well-being, such as job and retirement insecurity, health care costs, and spiraling college tuition. While one might expect that these concerns would motivate people to become more politically engaged on the issues, this often doesn't happen, and the resulting inaction carries consequences for political debates and public policy. Moving beyond previously studied barriers to political organization, American Insecurity sheds light on the public's inaction over economic insecurities by showing that the rhetoric surrounding these issues is actually self-undermining. By their nature, the very arguments intended to mobilize individuals--asking them to devote money or time to politics--remind citizens of their economic fears and personal constraints, leading to undermobilization and nonparticipation.Adam Seth Levine explains why the set of people who become politically active on financial insecurity issues is therefore quite narrow. When money is needed, only those who care about the issues but are not personally affected become involved. When time is needed, participation is limited to those not personally affected or those who are personally affected but outside of the labor force with time to spare. The latter explains why it is relatively easy to mobilize retirees on topics that reflect personal financial concerns, such as Social Security and Medicare. In general, however, when political representation requires a large group to make their case, economic insecurity threats are uniquely disadvantaged.Scrutinizing the foundations of political behavior, American Insecurity offers a new perspective on collective participation”--

Provided by publisher. Subjects: Finance, Personal--United States. Political participation--United States. Political Science / Public Policy / Economic Policy. Political Science / Political Process / General. Business & Economics / Personal Finance / General. Political Science / Political Process / Political Advocacy. United States--Economic conditions--21st century. United States--Economic policy--21st century. Notes: Includes bibliographical references (pages 283-296) and index.

Applied health economics LCCN: 2012006760 Main title: Applied health economics / Andrew M. Jones ... [et al.]. Edition: 2nd ed. Published/Created: New York: Routledge, 2013. Description: xx, 396 p.: ill.; 24 cm. ISBN: 9780415676816 (hbk) 9780415676823 (pbk.) 9780203102411 (ebk) LC classification: RA410.5 .A66 2013 Related names: Jones, Andrew M., 1960- Summary: "The first edition of Applied Health Economics did an expert job of showing how the availability of large scale data sets and the rapid advancement of advanced econometric techniques can help health economists and health professionals make sense of information better than ever before.The book draws on key sources of information such as the European Community Household Panel (ECHP) and the WHO Multi-Country Survey Study (WHO-MCS) and assumes a familiarity with the computer programme Stata, now in an eleventh version. The book has been fully updated to reflect the enhancements to this key package.In addition to methodology, the book also contains a brand new chapter on regression models for health care costs, thus broadening the book's readership to those working on risk adjustment and health technology appraisal. The text also fully reflects the very latest advances in the health economics field and the key journal literature"--Provided by publisher. Contents: Data and survey design -- Describing the dynamics of health -- Describing health care costs -- Reporting heterogeneity in health -- Health and lifestyles -- Smoking and mortality -- Health and retirement -- Health and wages -- Modelling the dynamics of health -- Non-response and attrition bias -- Models for count data -- Modelling health care costs. Subjects: Economics, Medical. Health Care Costs.

Statistics as Topic. Notes: Includes bibliographical references (p. [381]-387) and index.

Barriers to lower health care costs for workers and employers: hearing before the Subcommittee on Health, Employment, Labor and Pensions, Committee on Education and the Workforce, U.S. House of Representatives, One Hundred Twelfth Congress, second session, hearing held in Washington, DC, May 31, 2012. LCCN: 2012515286 Corporate name: United States. Congress. House. Committee on Education and the Workforce. Subcommittee on Health, Employment, Labor, and Pensions. Main title: Barriers to lower health care costs for workers and employers: hearing before the Subcommittee on Health, Employment, Labor and Pensions, Committee on Education and the Workforce, U.S. House of Representatives, One Hundred Twelfth Congress, second session, hearing held in Washington, DC, May 31, 2012. Published/Created: Washington: U.S. G.P.O.: For sale by the Supt. of Docs., U.S. G.P.O., 2012. Description: iii, 52 p.: ill.; 24 cm. LC classification: KF27 .E3395 2012b Subjects: Medical care--United States--Cost control. Medical economics--United States. Health insurance--United States--Cost control. Notes: Shipping list no.: 2013-0001-P. "Serial no. 112-62." Includes bibliographical references. Additional formats: Online version: United States. Congress. House. Committee on Education and the Workforce. Subcommittee on Health, Employment, Labor, and Pensions. Barriers to lower health care costs for workers and employers (OCoLC)809853386

Breaking the iron triangle: a prescription for controlling health care costs LCCN: 2012936753 Personal name: Duggan, Robert M. Main title: Breaking the iron triangle: a prescription for controlling health care costs / Robert M. Duggan. Published/Created: Maryland, MA: WISDOMWELL Press, 2012.

Budget Committee mid-session hearings fiscal year 2014: hearings before the Committee on the Budget, United States Senate, One Hundred Thirteenth Congress, first session. LCCN: 2014406071 Corporate name: United States. Congress. Senate. Committee on the Budget, author. Main title: Budget

Committee mid-session hearings fiscal year 2014: hearings before the Committee on the Budget, United States Senate, One Hundred Thirteenth Congress, first session. Published/Produced: [Washington, D.C.]: [U.S. Government Printing Office], [2013?] Description: iv, 776 pages: illustrations; 24 cm. LC classification: KF26 .B8 2013 Portion of title: Mid-session hearings fiscal year 2014: hearings before the Committee on the Budget, United States Senate, One Hundred Thirteenth Congress, first session Contents: February 13, 2013. The impact of federal budget decision [on] families and communities -- February 26, 2013. The impact of federal investments on people, communities, and long-term economic growth -- March 5, 2013. Reducing the deficit by eliminating wasteful spending in the tax code -- May 22, 2013. Supporting broad-based economic growth and fiscal responsibility through tax reform -- June 4, 2013. Fiscal and economic effects of austerity -- June 26, 2013. Investing in our future: the impact of federal budget decisions on children -- July 23, 2013. The impact of sequestration on national security and the economy -- July 30, 2013. Containing health care costs: recent progress and remaining challenges -- September 24, 2013. The impact of political uncertainty on jobs and the economy. Subjects: Budget--United States. Government spending policy--United States. Finance, Public--United States. Fiscal policy--United States. Taxation--United States. Budget deficits--United States. United States--Economic policy--2009- United States--Economic conditions--2009- Notes: Shipping list no.: 2014-0224-P. Includes bibliographical references. Additional formats: Also available via the Internet from the GPO Access web site. Address as of 06/30/14: http://purl.fdlp.gov/GPO/gpo49151; current access is available via PURL. Online version: United States. Congress. Senate. Committee on the Budget. Budget Committee mid-session hearings fiscal year 2014 (OCoLC)880351270 Series: S. hrg.; 113-229 United States. Congress. Senate. S. hrg.; 113-229.

Capturing social and behavioral domains and measures in electronic health records: phase 2 LCCN: 2014959444 Main title: Capturing social and behavioral domains and measures in electronic health records: phase 2 / Committee on the Recommended Social and Behavioral Domains and Measures for Electronic Health Records; Board on Population Health and Public Health Practice; Institute of Medicine of the National Academies. Published/Produced: Washington, D.C.: The National Academies Press, [2014] ©2014 Description: xxii, 351 pages; 23 cm. ISBN: 9780309312424 0309312426 LC classification: R864 .C372 2014 Related names: Institute of Medicine (U.S.). Board on Population Health and Public Health Practice, issuing body. Summary: "Determinants of health - like physical activity levels and living conditions - have traditionally been the concern of public health and have not been linked closely to clinical practice. However, if standardized social and behavioral data can be incorporated into patient electronic health records (EHRs), those data can provide crucial information about factors that influence health and the effectiveness of treatment. Such information is useful for diagnosis, treatment choices, policy, health care system design, and innovations to improve health outcomes and reduce health care costs. Capturing Social and Behavioral Domains and Measures in Electronic Health Records: Phase 2 identifies domains and measures that capture the social determinants of health to inform the development of recommendations for the meaningful use of EHRs. This report is the second part of a two-part study. The Phase 1 report identified 17 domains for inclusion in EHRs. This report pinpoints 12 measures related to 11 of the initial domains and considers the implications of incorporating them into all EHRs. This book includes three chapters from the Phase 1 report in addition to the new Phase 2 material. Standardized use of EHRs that include social and behavioral domains could provide better patient care, improve population health, and enable more informative research. The recommendations of Capturing Social and Behavioral Domains and Measures in Electronic Health Records: Phase 2 will provide valuable information on which to base problem identification, clinical diagnoses, patient treatment, outcomes assessment, and population health measurement."-- Publisher's description. Contents: Selection of Domains for Consideration -- Identified Candidate Domains -- Measures Reviewed for Each Candidate Domain -- Recommended Core Domains and Measures -- Implementation Issues -- Looking Toward the Future -- Appendix A: Domains Reviewed But Not Selected for the Candidate Set -- Appendix B: Privacy Concerns Related to Inclusion of Social and Behavioral Determinants of Health in Electronic Health Records -- Appendix C: Agendas of Public Meetings -- Appendix D: Committee Biographies. Subjects: Medical records--Data processing. Drugs--Prescribing--Data processing. Additional formats: Also available online. Online version: Institute of Medicine (U.S.). Committee on the Recommended Social and Behavioral Domains and Measures for Electronic Health Records. Capturing social and behavioral domains in electronic health records. Washington, D.C.: National Academies Press, 2014 (OCoLC)900016777

Catastrophic care: why everything we think we know about health care is wrong LCCN: 2014378470 Personal name: Goldhill, David, author. Main title: Catastrophic care: why everything we think we know about health care is wrong / David Goldhill. Edition: First Vintage Books edition. Published/Produced: New York: Vintage Books, a division of Random House LLC, 2013. Description: xxviii, 385 pages; 21 cm ISBN: 9780345802736 (pbk.) 034580273X (pbk.) LC classification: RA410.53 .G655 2013b Subjects: Medical care, Cost of--United States. Health insurance--United States. Health services accessibility--United States. Medical errors--United States. Health Care Costs--United States. Insurance, Health--United States. Health Services Accessibility--United States. Medical Errors--United States. Notes: Originally published by Alfred A. Knopf, 2013. Includes bibliographical references (pages 357-369) and index.

Changing the U.S. health care system: key issues in health services policy and management LCCN: 2013013537 Main title: Changing the U.S. health care system: key issues in health services policy and management / Gerald F. Kominski, editor. Edition: 4th ed. Published/Created: San Francisco: Jossey-Bass, c2014. Description: lvi, 784 p.: ill.; 25

cm. ISBN: 9781118128916 (cloth) LC classification: RA395.A3 C478 2014 Related names: Kominski, Gerald F. Contents: Changing the U.S. health care system: the patient protection and affordable care act -- Improving access to care in America -- Ethnic disparities in health status -- Racial and ethnic disparities in health care - - Multilevel social determinants of health -- Public policies to extend health care coverage -- Private health insurance -- Measuring health care costs and trends -- Containing health care costs -- Promoting pharmaceutical access while controlling prices and expenditures -- Measuring health-related quality of life and other outcomes -- Evaluating the quality of care -- Public release of information on quality -- Health care information systems -- Performance measurement of nursing care -- Long-term services and supports for the elderly population -- HIV and AIDs in the twenty-first century -- Health reform for children and families -- Homeless persons -- Changing the US health care delivery system -- Medicare reform -- Public health and clinical care -- Strengthening the safety net -- Ethical issues in public health and health services. Subjects: Health Care Reform--United States. Delivery of Health Care--United States. Health Policy--United States. Notes: Includes bibliographical references and index. Additional formats: Online version: Changing the U.S. health care system 4th ed. San Francisco: Jossey-Bass, c2014 9781118418901 (DLC) 2013014356

Comparative effectiveness research: evidence, medicine, and policy LCCN: 2013006780 Personal name: Ashton, Carol M. Main title: Comparative effectiveness research: evidence, medicine, and policy / Carol M. Ashton, Nelda P. Wray. Published/Created: Oxford; New York: Oxford University Press, c2013. Description: xiii, 290 p.; 25 cm. ISBN: 9780199968565 (hardback: alk. paper) 019996856X (hardback: alk. paper) 9780199969579 (e-book) 0199969574 (e-book) LC classification: RA440.87.U6 A84 2013 Related names: Wray, Nelda P. Contents: The generation of evidence in medicine: evaluating the benefits and harms of treatment -- The use of evidence: federal regulation of prescription drugs and medical devices -- The subversion of evidence: the

Rosiglitazone story -- Operate first, evidence later: the special case of surgery -- Doctors and evidence: evidence-based medicine -- Comparative effective research: a new "silver bullet" for U.S. health care costs -- The legislative odyssey of comparative effectiveness research: birth in 2002 to the first federal mandate in 2003 -- 2005 to 2007: the health services research community stirs, the "B" word awakens policymakers, and the House CHAMP Act creates divisions -- 2008 to 2010: the Baucus-Conrad bills, the American Recovery and Reinvestment Act, and the Patient Protection and Affordable Care Act -- The scope, financing, and processes of federally-mandated comparative effectiveness research and why they matter -- Aligning clinical practice with best evidence of comparative effectiveness: payment policy for evidence-based medical care -- Dealing with uncertainty: payment policy for the generation of evidence as part of clinical practice. Subjects: Medical care--Research--United States--Evaluation. Evidence-based medicine--United States. Medical care, Cost of--Law and legislation--United States. Medical policy--United States. Comparative Effectiveness Research--history--United States. Health Care Costs--legislation & jurisprudence--United States. Comparative Effectiveness Research--legislation & jurisprudence--United States. Evidence-Based Medicine--United States. Government Regulation--United States. History, 21st Century--United States. Notes: Includes bibliographical references and index.

Core measurement needs for better care, better health, and lower costs: counting what counts: workshop summary LCCN: 2013372291 Meeting name: Core Metrics for Better Care, Better Health, and Lower Costs (Workshop) (2012: Irvine, Calif.) Main title: Core measurement needs for better care, better health, and lower costs: counting what counts: workshop summary / Joe Alper, Julia Sanders, and Robert Saunders, rapporteurs; Roundtable on Value & Science-Driven Health Care; Institute of Medicine of the National Academies. Published/Produced: Washington, D.C.: National Academies Press, [2013] ©2013 Description: xx, 128 pages: illustrations; 23 cm. Links: National Academies Press http://www.nap.edu/catalog.php ?record_id=18333 ISBN: 0309285224 (pbk.) 9780309285223 (pbk.) LC classification: RA410.53 .C676 2012 Related names: Alper, Joe, reporter. Sanders, Julia (Julia C.), reporter. Saunders, Robert Samuel, 1978- reporter. Institute of Medicine (U.S.). Roundtable on Value & Science-Driven Health Care, issuing body. Contents: Vision -- Current measurement capabilities -- Core metrics sets in use -- Specifying the shape of a core metrics set -- Implementation -- Building the infrastructure -- Common themes. Subjects: Medical care, Cost of--United States--Evaluation--Congresses. Medical care--United States--Cost control--Congresses. Medical care--United States--Evaluation--Congresses. Medical policy--United States--Congresses. Outcome Assessment (Health Care)--United States--Congresses. Quality Assurance, Health Care--United States--Congresses. Health Care Costs--United States--Congresses. Health Status--United States--Congresses. Quality of Health Care--United States--Congresses. Costs and Cost Analysis--United States--Congresses. Health Policy--United States--Congresses. Notes: A report on the proceedings of a workshop held by the Roundtable on Value & Science-Driven Health Care of the Institute of Medicine at the Beckman Center of the National Academies, 100 Academy Way, Irvine, California, December 5-6, 2012. Includes bibliographical references. Additional formats: Online version: Core measurement needs for basic care, better health, and lower costs. Washington, D.C.: National Academies Press, 2013 9780309285223 (OCoLC)852522866. Series: The learning health system series

Creating evidence for better health financing decisions: a strategic guide for the institutionalization of national health accounts LCCN: 2011048884 Main title: Creating evidence for better health financing decisions: a strategic guide for the institutionalization of national health accounts / Akiko Maeda ... [et al.]. Published/Created: Washington DC: World Bank, c2012. Description: xxxviii, 344 p.: ill.; 23 cm. ISBN: 9780821394694 (pbk.: alk. paper) 9780821394700 (e-ISBN) LC classification: RA395.D44 C74 2012 Related names: Maeda, Akiko. World Bank. Contents: The case for institutionalizing national health accounts -- Governance structures for NHA -- Building capacity to sustain NHA activities -- Financing strategy for NHA -- Translation and dissemination of NHA -- The value of global and regional partners. Subjects: National Health Programs--economics. Delivery of Health Care--economics. Developing Countries. Economics, Medical. Health Care Costs. Notes: Includes bibliographical references. Series: Directions in development (Washington, D.C.) Directions in development (Washington, D.C.)

Cries of crisis: rethinking the health care debate LCCN: 2012017298 Personal name: Hackey, Robert B. Main title: Cries of crisis: rethinking the health care debate / Robert B. Hackey. Published/Created: Reno, Nevada: University of Nevada Press, c2012. Description: xi, 174 p.; 24 cm. ISBN: 9780874178890 (cloth: alk. paper) 0874178894 (cloth: alk. paper) LC classification: RA395.A3 H33 2012 Variant title: Rethinking the health care debate Contents: The rhetoric of health care reform -- The cost crisis -- The medical malpractice crisis -- The nurse staffing crisis -- The health insurance crisis. Subjects: Health Care Reform--United States. Health Care Costs--United States. Health Policy--United States. Insurance, Health--United States. Malpractice--United States. Nurses--supply & distribution--United States. Notes: Includes bibliographical references (p. 161-170) and index.

Decision-making in nursing: thoughtful approaches for leadership LCCN: 2013049711 Main title: Decision-making in nursing: thoughtful approaches for leadership / edited by Sandra B. Lewenson, EdD, RN, FAAN, Professor of Nursing, College of Health Professions, Lienhard School of Nursing, Pace University, Pleasantville, New York, Marie Truglio-Londrigan, PhD, RN, Professor of Nursing, College of Health Professions, Lienhard School of Nursing, Pace University, Pleasantville, New York. Edition: Second edition. Published/Produced: Burlington, MA: Jones & Bartlett Learning, [2015] Description: xxvi, 254 pages: illustrations; 23 cm ISBN: 9781284026177 (pbk.) LC classification: RT42 .D433 2015 Related names: Lewenson,

Sandra, editor of compilation. Truglio-Londrigan, Marie, editor of compilation. Contents: Know yourself: reflective decision-making -- Looking back: history and decision-making in health care -- Right or wrong: policy, legal and ethical issues and decision-making -- More than prayer: spirituality and decision-making -- Culture and decision making -- Family and decision-making -- Media and decision-making -- Working together: team, group, & coalition decision-making -- Evidence-based decision-making -- Health care costs matter: economics and decision making -- Getting involved: public policy and influencing the outcomes -- Use of technology for decision-making. Subjects: Decision Making. Nursing Care--methods. Leadership. Notes: Includes bibliographical references and index.

Delivering Affordable Cancer Care in the 21st Century: workshop summary LCCN: 2013444474 Meeting name: Delivering Affordable Cancer Care in the 21st Century (Workshop) (2012: Washington, D.C.), author. Main title: Delivering Affordable Cancer Care in the 21st Century: workshop summary / Erin Balogh, Margie Patlak, and Sharyl J. Nass, rapporteurs; National Cancer Policy Forum, Board on Health Care Services, Institute of Medicine of the National Academies. Published/Produced: Washington, D.C.: National Academies Press, [2013] ©2013 Description: xiv, 80 pages: illustrations (some color), color map; 24 cm ISBN: 9780309269445 (pbk.) 030926944X (pbk.) LC classification: RC270.8 .D45 2013 Related names: Balogh, Erin. Patlak, Margie. Nass, Sharyl J. National Cancer Policy Forum (U.S.), sponsoring body. Institute of Medicine (U.S.). Board on Health Care Services, issuing body. Summary: "Rising health care costs are a central fiscal challenge confronting the United States. National spending on health care currently accounts for 18 percent of gross domestic product (GDP), but is anticipated to increase to 25 percent of GDP by 2037. The Bipartisan Policy Center argues that "this rapid growth in health expenditures creates an unsustainable burden on America's economy, with far-reaching consequences." These consequences include crowding out many national priorities, including investments in education, infrastructure, and research; stagnation of employee wages; and decreased international competitiveness. In spite of health care costs that far exceed those of other countries, health outcomes in the United States are not considerably better. With the goal of ensuring that patients have access to high-quality, affordable cancer care, the Institute of Medicine's (IOM's) National Cancer Policy Forum convened a public workshop, Delivering Affordable Cancer Care in the 21st Century, October 8-9, 2012, in Washington, DC. Delivering Affordable Cancer Care in the 21st Century summarizes the workshop"-- Publisher's description. Contents: Introduction -- A financial crisis in health care -- Drivers of health care costs -- Cancer care costs -- Financial burden on patients with cancer -- Questionable value -- Current challenges -- Inappropriate incentives -- Unrealistic expectations -- Overuse and misuse of interventions -- Variable care, lack of best practices, and an inadequate evidence base -- Legal and regulatory issues -- Assessing value -- Possible solutions -- Patient and clinician communication and education -- Best practices in cancer care -- Evidence base for clinical practice and reimbursement -- Financial incentives aligned with affordable, high-quality cancer care -- Delivery system and reimbursement changes -- Wrap up. Subjects: Cancer--Treatment--Congresses. Medical care, Cost of--Congresses. Medical care--Finance--Congresses. Health Care Costs--United States--Congresses. Neoplasms--therapy--United States--Congresses. Evidence-Based Medicine--United States--Congresses. Health Services--economics--United States--Congresses. Neoplasms--economics--United States--Congresses. Practice Guidelines as Topic--United States--Congresses. Notes: Includes bibliographical references (pages 67-74).

Examining the lifetime costs of supporting the newest generation of veterans: hearing before the Committee on Veterans' Affairs, United States Senate, One Hundred Twelfth Congress, first session, July 27, 2011. LCCN: 2011487576 Corporate name: United States. Congress. Senate. Committee on Veterans' Affairs. Main title: Examining the lifetime costs of supporting the newest generation of veterans: hearing before the Committee on

Veterans' Affairs, United States Senate, One Hundred Twelfth Congress, first session, July 27, 2011. Published/Created: Washington: U.S. G.P.O.: For sale by the Supt. of Docs., U.S. G.P.O., 2012. Description: iii, 77 p.: ill.; 24 cm. Links: PDF version: http://purl.fdlp.gov/GPO/gpo19579 ISBN: 9780160903922 0160903920 LC classification: KF26 .V4 2011d Subjects: United States. Department of Veterans Affairs--Appropriations and expenditures. Veterans--Medical care--United States--Costs--Forecasting. Medical care, Cost of--United States. Forecasting. Health Care Costs--United States. Veterans Health--economics--United States. Notes: Shipping list no.: 2012-0181-P. Includes bibliographical references. Reproduction no./Source: 552-070-44058-5 GPO Additional formats: Also available via the Internet from the GPO Access web site. Address as of 04/12/12: http://purl.fdlp.gov/GPO/gpo19579; current access is available via PURL. Online version: United States. Congress. Senate. Committee on Veterans' Affairs. Examining the lifetime costs of supporting the newest generation of veterans (OCoLC)779349618 Series: S. hrg.; 112-236 United States. Congress. Senate. S. hrg.; 112-236.

Executing lean improvements: a practical guide with real-world healthcare case studies LCCN: 2015007112 Personal name: Delisle, Dennis R., 1984- , author. Main title: Executing lean improvements: a practical guide with real-world healthcare case studies / Dennis R. Delisle. Published/Produced: Milwaukee, Wisconsin: ASQ Quality Press, [2015] Description: xxvii, 245 pages: illustrations (some color); 26 cm. + 1 CD-ROM (4 3/4 in.) ISBN: 9780873899093 (hbk: alk. paper) LC classification: R728 .D45 2015 Related names: American Society for Quality, issuing body. Subjects: Thomas Jefferson University. Cost Control--methods--Pennsylvania. Health Care Costs--Pennsylvania. Organizational Case Studies--Pennsylvania. Quality Improvement--economics--Pennsylvania. Notes: Includes bibliographical references and index.

Five steps to a successful workplace wellness program: a RAND toolkit LCCN: 2014497635 Personal name: Van Busum,

Kristin R., author. Main title: Five steps to a successful workplace wellness program: a RAND toolkit / Kristin R. Van Busum, Hangsheng Liu, Soeren Mattke. Published/Created: Santa Monica, CA: RAND Corp., c2014. Description: 27 p.: col. ill.; 28 cm. Links: Related Electronic Resource: Publisher's web page for this work, including summary from back cover, and link to scanned depiction of full text and images: http://www.rand.org/pubs/tools/TL141.html ISBN: 9780833086860 (pbk.) LC classification: RC969.H43 V36 2014 Variant title: 5 steps to a successful workplace wellness program Portion of title: Workplace wellness program Related names: Liu, Hangsheng, author. Mattke, Soeren, author. Rand Corporation, issuing body. RAND Health, issuing body. Summary: "Well-designed, well-executed workplace wellness programs can reduce health risks (such as smoking and physical inactivity), lower health care costs, and improve productivity. RAND researchers determined that these programs are becoming a standard component of benefits packages but that not all of them are created equal: Some generate cost savings whereas others do not, and there are substantial differences in how programs are being designed and implemented. This toolkit synthesizes the lessons learned and best practices from multiple projects and many years of research into a five-step guide for the planning, implementation, and evaluation of a successful workplace wellness program."-- Summary from page 4 of cover. Subjects: Employee health promotion--Handbooks, manuals, etc. Preventive health services--Handbooks, manuals, etc. Health promotion--Planning--Handbooks, manuals, etc. Health services administration Handbooks, manuals, etc. Industrial hygiene--Handbooks, manuals, etc. Work environment--United States. Notes: "RAND Corporation tool series."--Web page (PDF). "The work was conducted in RAND Health"--Verso of title page. "TL-141"--Page 4 of cover.

Fundamentals of retiree group benefits LCCN: 2015013481 Personal name: Yamamoto, Dale H., 1952- Main title: Fundamentals of retiree group benefits / Dale H. Yamamoto. Edition: Second Edition. Published/Produced: Winsted, CT: ACTEX Publications, Inc., 2015. Description: pages cm

ISBN: 9781625424839 (alk. paper) LC classification: HQ1063.2.U6 Y36 2015 Summary: "Retiree group benefits continue to have the reputation for being difficult to understand. This book attempts to provide a fundamental understanding of almost all of the elements that make up the world of retiree group benefits"-- Provided by publisher. Contents: Preface -- Introduction -- Erosion of retiree health benefits -- Medicare -- Retiree benefit design -- Funding -- Legal issues -- U.S. private sector accounting -- Other accounting -- Actuarial methods and assumptions -- Appendix a retiree group benefit design A -- Appendix B medicare part D B -- Appendix C key IRS code and regulations C -- Appendix D cases regarding retiree health care D -- Appendix E Health care costs by age E -- Appendix F Health practice note 2006 F -- Appendix G ASOP G -- Appendix H commutation functions H- -- Bibliography -- Index. Subjects: Retirees--United States. Postemployment benefits--United States. Group insurance--United States. Notes: Includes bibliographical references and index.

Handbook of musculoskeletal pain and disability disorders in the workplace LCCN: 2014936415 Main title: Handbook of musculoskeletal pain and disability disorders in the workplace / Robert J. Gatchel, Izabela Z. Schultz, editors. Published/Produced: New York: Springer, [2014] ©2014 Description: xvi, 509 pages: illustrations, map; 26 cm ISBN: 9781493906116 (hbk: alk. paper) 1493906119 (hbk: alk. paper) LC classification: RB127.5.C48 H36 2014 Related names: Gatchel, Robert J., 1947- editor. Schultz, Izabela Z., 1951- editor. Summary: Chronic pain from job-related stressors is responsible for countless lost work hours and considerable lost revenue--and if current statistics are any indication, the problem isn't going away anytime soon. Between rising numbers of affected workers and rising health care costs, musculoskeletal pain has taken on crisis proportions. The Handbook of Musculoskeletal Pain and Disability Disorders in the Workplace addresses the complex state of the issues in authoritative and practical fashion. Divided evenly between common occupational pain disorders, conceptual and methodological issues, and evidence-based intervention methods, this comprehensive reference presents current findings on prevalence, causation, and physical and psychosocial aspects common to these disorders. Attention is given to working-world concerns, including insurance and compensation issues and AMA guidelines for disability evaluations. Also, specialized chapters offer lenses for understanding and administering the best approaches for treating specific pain disorders, as well as explore what workplaces can do to accommodate affected employees and prevent injuries from occurring in the first place. The Handbook of musculoskeletal pain and disability disorders in the workplace offers expert, up-to-date coverage suited to health psychologists, rehabilitation specialists (including physical, vocational, and occupational therapists), human resources and disability management professionals, and occupational medicine physicians. -- Back Cover Contents: Part 1 The most common occupational musculoskeletal pain and disability disorders -- 1. Occupational musculoskeletal pain and disability disorders: an overview / Robert J. Gatchel, Nancy D. Kishino, and Alan M. Strizak -- 2. Back pain / Andrew R. Block and Jessica Shellock -- 3. Cervical pain / John C. Alexander, Humair Rana, and William Epps -- 4. Upper extremity pain / Jean-Sébastien Roy, Kadija Perreault, and Francois Desmeules -- 5. Lower extremity pain / Krista Howard, David March, Haseeb Ikram, Jenna Lorentsen, and Jeffrey Howard -- 6. Chronic widespread pain and fibromyalgia syndrome / Akiko Okifuji and Bradford D. Hare -- 7. The problem of whiplash injuries: aetiology, assessment and treatment / Michele Sterling -- 8. New trends of musculoskeletal disorders in the military / Cindy A. McGeary and Donald D. McGeary -- Part II Conceptual and methodological issues -- 9. Search Engines and resources available to obtain the latest incidence and cost data for occupational pain and disability disorders / Brian R. Theodore -- 10. Epidemiology of musculoskeletal disorders and workplace factors / J. Mark Melhorn -- 11. From acute pain to chronic disability: psychosocial processes in the development of chronic musculoskeletal pain and disability / K. Boersma, J.

Carstens-Söderstrand, and S. J. Linton -- 12. Psychosocial and psychiatric sequelae of chronic musculoskeletal pain and disability disorders / Robert J. Gatchel and Angela Liegey Dougall -- 13. Pre-employment and preplacement screening for workers to prevent occupational musculoskeletal disorders / Matthew T. Knauf, Sali R. Asih, and Glenn Pransky -- 14. Disability and impairment in medicolegal settings: pain disability controversies / Izabela Z. Schultz and Catherine M. Chlebak -- 15. Workers' compensation and other disability insurance systems involved in occupational musculoskeletal disorders / Richard C. Robinson and John P. Garofalo -- 16. Approaches to the quantitative physical and functional capacity assessment of occupational musculoskeletal disorders / Samuel M. Bierner -- 17. Current American Medical Association guidelines for evaluating musculoskeletal impairment at maximum medical improvement / Robert Rondinelli and Mohammed Ranavaya -- Part III Intervention approaches and techniques -- 18. Traditional medical intervention approaches to musculoskeletal disorders: a review / Stephanie Jones -- 19. The biopsychosocial approach to the assessment and intervention for people with musculoskeletal disorders / Dennis C. Turk -- 20. The interdisciplinary treatment approach for chronic pain management: the key components for success / Ben Lippe and Peter B. Polatin -- 21. Early intervention to prevent the development of chronic musculoskeletal pain disorders and disability / Robert J. Gatchel, Nancy D. Kishino, and Izabela Z. Schultz -- 22. A review of self-management support for (work-related) musculoskeletal pain disorders / Niki Ellis, Dianne M. Sheppard, Malcolm Battersby, and Fiona J. Clay -- 23. Work accommodation in musculoskeletal disorders: current challenges and future directions in research and practice / Hanah C. Kwan and Izabela Z. Schultz -- 24. Models of return to work for musculoskeletal disorders: advances in conceptualization and research / Matthew T. Knauf, Izabela Z. Schultz, Alison M. Stewart, and Robert J. Gatchel -- 25. Vocational assessment and training for patients with chronic occupational musculoskeletal disorders / Kelly Chapman, Robert Lisson, and Ben Haynes

-- 26. Real-effectiveness medicine in musculoskeletal disorders / Antti O.V. Malmivaara -- 27. Future research directions for preventing and treating occupational musculoskeletal disorders / Robert J. Gatchel and Izabela Z. Schultz -- Index. Subjects: Chronic pain--Handbooks, manuals, etc. People with disabilities--Employment--Handbooks, manuals, etc. Industrial hygiene--Handbooks, manuals, etc. Musculoskeletal Pain. Disability Evaluation. Occupational Diseases. Chronic pain. Industrial hygiene. People with disabilities--Employment. Form/Genre: Handbooks, manuals, etc. Notes: Includes bibliographical references and index. Series: Handbooks in health, work, and disability, 2198-7084

Health care finance, economics, and policy for nurses: a foundational guide LCCN: 2014049307 Personal name: Rambur, Betty, author. Main title: Health care finance, economics, and policy for nurses: a foundational guide / Betty Rambur. Published/Produced: New York: Springer Publishing Company, LLC, [2015] Description: p.; cm. ISBN: 9780826123220 LC classification: RT86.7 Contents: What is health economics and why is it important to nurses? -- A story of unintended consequences: how economic and policy solutions create new challenges -- Payment reform -- How health care markets differ from classic free markets -- The role of information in health care markets and decision making -- Market entry, exit, and antitrust law -- What is ethiconomics? -- Additional models to guide ethical decision-making -- Governance and organizational types -- Applying health economics to influence health care through state and federal policy formation -- Epilogue: reflections on living and leading in a changing nursing world. Subjects: Healthcare Financing--Nurses' Instruction. Healthcare Financing--Problems and Exercises. Decision Making--Nurses' Instruction. Decision Making--Problems and Exercises. Health Care Costs--Nurses' Instruction. Health Care Costs--Problems and Exercises. Health Policy--Nurses' Instruction. Health Policy--Problems and Exercises. Notes: Includes bibliographical references and index.

Health care LCCN: 2011048764 Main title: Health care / Noël

Merino, book editor. Published/Created: Farmington Hills, MI: Greenhaven Press, c2012. Description: 230 p.: ill., maps; 24 cm. ISBN: 9780737756548 (hardcover) 0737756543 (hardcover) 9780737756555 (pbk.) 0737756551 (pbk.) LC classification: RA411 .H415 2012 Related names: Merino, Noël. Contents: ch. 1. Access to health care around the globe. In developed countries, most people have access to health care / Organisation for Economic Co-operation and Development (OECD) -- In the United States, a new law will help lessen the high number of uninsured / Kaiser Family Foundation -- In Canada, wait times for health care are unacceptably long / Bacchus Barua and Mark Rovere -- In India, there is vast inequality in access to health care / Y. Balarajan, S. Selvaraj, and S.V. Subramanian -- In China, there is a plan to reduce the millions without health care / Veronica M. Valdez -- In South Africa, migrants do not have adequate access to health care / Human Rights Watch -- ch. 2. The quality of health care. Health care in the United States is superior in many categories / Scott W. Atlas -- The health care experience in France is better than in the United States / Matt Welch -- The national health service in Great Britain needs reform / Spectator (UK) -- Cuba's health care system works well in Cuba and elsewhere / Sarah van Gelder -- Beyond hysterics: the health care model that works / Anita Raghavan -- In Brazil, health care is universal but not necessarily high quality / Jeb Blount -- ch. 3. The cost of health care. In Europe, health care costs are rising faster than available funding / Economist Intelligence Unit -- Australia should emulate Singapore to control rising health care costs / Richard Harper -- Canada's single-payer system controls costs better than America's system / Diane Francis -- Taiwan's health care system delivers quality with low costs / Ian Williams -- In Africa, fees for health care keep people from seeking treatment / Oxfam International -- ch. 4. Disease-related challenges for health care. Despite some progress, HIV remains a global health challenge / Joint United Nations Programme on HIV/AIDS (UNAIDS) -- The worldwide fight against malaria is far from over / Jeremy Laurance -- Drug-resistant tuberculosis poses a global health threat / Jeneen Interlandi -- India on the front lines in the battle to eradicate polio / Stephanie Nolen -- Infectious diseases in the developing world remain a serious problem / International Federation of Red Cross and Red Crescent Societies (IFRC) -- Cancer is a growing health problem, especially in the developing world / Margaret Chan and Yukiya Amano. Subjects: Medical care. Health services accessibility. Communicable diseases--Prevention. Human rights. Notes: Includes bibliographical references and index. Series: Global viewpoints Global viewpoints.

Health reforms in Central and Eastern Europe since 1990: comparative context and concerns / James Warner Björkman -- 2. Health reforms in Armenia, 1990-2010 / Lianna Mkhitaryan -- 3. Health reforms in Bulgaria / T. Kostadinova [and 3 others] -- 4. Health reforms in the Czech Republic / Ivan Malý, Marek Pavlik and Zuzana Darmopilová -- 5. Health policy in Hungary / Sándor Gallai -- 6. Health system reforms in the Republic of Macedonia, 1991-2010 / Vladimir Lazarevik [and 3 others] -- 7. Health reforms in Romania / Răzvan Cherecheş -- Patterns of health care reform in economies under transition: the case of Russia / Tatiana Chubarova and Natalia Grigorieva -- 9. Health reforms in Slovakia / Juraj Nemec -- 10. The health care system in Slovakia / Stanka Setnikar-Cankar and Veronika Petkovšek -- Observations, inferences and conclusions / Juraj Nemec. Subjects: Health care reform--Europe, Central. Health care reform--Europe, Eastern. Medical care, Cost of--Europe, Central. Medical care, Cost of--Europe, Eastern. Medical policy--Europe, Central. Medical policy--Europe, Eastern. Health Care Reform--Europe, Eastern. Health Care Costs--Europe, Eastern. Health Policy--Europe, Eastern. Health care reform. Medical care, Cost of. Medical policy. Europe, Central. Europe, Eastern. Notes: Includes bibliographical references. Additional formats: Online version: Health reforms in Central and Eastern Europe. The Hague: Eleven International Pub., 2013 9789460947698 (OCoLC)859158896

Health reforms in Central and Eastern Europe: options, obstacles, limited outcomes LCCN: 2012276149 Main title: Health reforms in Central and

Eastern Europe: options, obstacles, limited outcomes / [edited by] James Warner Björkman & Juraj Nemec. Published/Produced: The Hague: Eleven International Publishing, [2013] Description: x, 296 pages: illustrations; 24 cm ISBN: 9789462360631 (pbk.) 9462360634 (pbk.) 9789460947698 (e-book) 9460947697 (e-book) LC classification: RA395.E85 H395 2013 Related names: Bjorkman, James Warner, editor. Nemec, Juraj, editor. Summary: Given dramatic changes in Central and Eastern Europe since the fall of Berlin Wall 1989 and the dissolution of the Soviet Union in 1991, local area experts were challenged to examine their national systems of health care as well as proposals to reform them. Each chapter provides contextual data and information on the empirical realities of a specific country at five-year intervals since 1990 as well as the organizational framework of its health care system. The book explores the historical thread of reforms attempted and their current state of implementation by addressing criteria for reforming national health systems such as costs, effectiveness, efficiency, equity and feasibility. The authors stress selected policy elements such as the roles of major actors, the shadow economy, cost containment, access, centralization and decentralization. While no blueprint is offered, intriguing patterns emerge across the cases plus observations about 'next steps' in the unfolding process of health reforms in the region. - Source other than Library of Congress. Contents

High prices, low transparency: the bitter pill of health care costs: hearing before the Committee on Finance, United States Senate, One Hundred Thirteenth Congress, first session, June 18, 2013. LCCN: 2014406942 Corporate name: United States. Congress. Senate. Committee on Finance, author. Main title: High prices, low transparency: the bitter pill of health care costs: hearing before the Committee on Finance, United States Senate, One Hundred Thirteenth Congress, first session, June 18, 2013. Published/Produced: Washington: U.S. Government Printing Office, 2013. Washington, DC: For sale by the Superintendent of Documents, U.S. Government Printing Office Description: iii, 158 pages: illustrations; 24 cm. LC classification: KF26 .F5 2013r

Subjects: Medical care, Cost of--United States. Medical care--United States--Cost control. Medical fees--United States. Form/Genre: Legislative hearings. Notes: Shipping list no.: 2014-0228-P. Includes bibliographical references. Additional formats: Online version: United States. Congress. Senate. Committee on Finance. High prices, low transparency (OCoLC)879175290 Microfiche version: United States. Congress. Senate. Committee on Finance. High prices, low transparency (OCoLC)890320865 Series: S. hrg.; 113-243 United States. Congress. Senate. S. hrg.; 113-243.

Introduction to health care management LCCN: 2011013461 Main title: Introduction to health care management / edited by Sharon Buchbinder, Nancy Shanks. Edition: 2nd ed. Published/Created: Burlington, Mass.: Jones & Bartlett Learning, c2012. Description: xxx, 494 p.: ill.; 24 cm. ISBN: 9780763790868 (pbk.) 0763790869 (pbk.) LC classification: RA971 .I58 2012 Related names: Buchbinder, Sharon Bell. Shanks, Nancy H. Contents: An overview of health care management / Jon M. Thompson, Sharon B. Buchbinder, Nancy H. Shanks -- Leadership / Louis Rubino -- Management and motivation / Nancy H. Shanks, Amy Dore -- Organizational behavior and management thinking / Sheila K. McGinnis -- Strategic planning / Susan Judd Casciani -- Healthcare marketing / Ruth Chavez, Nancy Sayre -- Quality improvement basics / Eric S. Williams, Grant T. Savage, Dennis G. Stambaugh -- Information technology / Tressa Springmann -- Financing health care and health insurance / Nancy H. Shanks -- Managing costs and revenues / Kevin D. Zeiler -- Managing healthcare professionals / Sharon B. Buchbinder, Dale Buchbinder -- The strategic management of human resources / Jon M. Thompson -- Teamwork / Sharon B. Buchbinder, Jon M. Thompson -- Addressing health disparities: cultural proficiency / Nancy Sayre, Ruth Chavez -- Ethics and law / Kevin D. Zeiler -- Fraud and abuse / Kevin D. Zeiler -- Healthcare management guidelines and case studies / Sharon B. Buchbinder, Donna M. Cox, Susan Judd Casciani. Subjects: Health services administration. Health Services

Administration. Efficiency, Organizational. Health Care Costs. Leadership. Organizational Case Studies. Notes: Includes bibliographical references and index.

Introduction to health care management LCCN: 2015040132 Main title: Introduction to health care management / [edited by] Sharon B. Buchbinder and Nancy H. Shanks. Edition: Third edition. Published/Produced: Burlington, Massachusetts: Jones & Bartlett Learning, [2015] Description: p.; cm. ISBN: 9781284081015 (paper) LC classification: RA971 Related names: Buchbinder, Sharon Bell, editor. Shanks, Nancy H., editor. Contents: An overview of health care management -- Leadership -- Management and motivation -- Organizational behavior and management thinking -- Strategic planning -- Healthcare marketing -- Quality improvement basics -- Information technology -- Financing health care and health insurance -- Managing costs and revenues -- Managing health care professionals -- The strategic management of human resources -- Teamwork -- Addressing health disparities: cultural proficiency -- Ethics and law -- Fraud and abuse -- Special topics and emerging issues in health care management -- Healthcare management case studies and guidelines. Subjects: Health Services Administration. Efficiency, Organizational. Health Care Costs. Leadership. Notes: Includes bibliographical references and index.

Jonas and Kovner's health care delivery in the United States LCCN: 2014045558 Main title: Jonas and Kovner's health care delivery in the United States / [edited by] James R. Knickman, Anthony R. Kovner. Edition: 11th edition. Published/Produced: New York: Springer Publishing Company, LLC, [2015] Description: p.; cm. ISBN: 9780826125279 LC classification: RA395.A3 Variant title: Health care delivery in the United States Related names: Knickman, James, editor. Kovner, Anthony R., editor. Contents: The challenge of health care delivery and health policy / James R. Knickman and Anthony R. Kovner -- An overview in charts / Catherine K. Dangremond -- Government and health insurance: the policy process / Michael S. Sparer and Frank J.

Thompson -- Comparative health systems / Michael K. Gusmano and Victor G. Rodwin -- Population health / Pamela Russo -- Public health: a transformation for the 21st century / Laura C. Leviton, Paul L. Kuehnert, and Kathryn E. Wehr -- Health and behavior / Elaine F. Cassidy, Matthew D. Trujillo, and C. Tracy Orleans -- Vulnerable populations: a tale of two nations / Jacqueline Martinez Garcel, Elizabeth A. Ward, and Lourdes J. Rodríguez -- Organization of care / Amy Yarbrough Landry and Cathleen O. Erwin -- The health workforcc / Joannc Spctz and Susan A. Chapman -- Health care financing / James R. Knickman -- Health care costs and value / Thad Calabrese and Keith F. Safian -- High-quality health care / Carolyn M. Clancy and Irene Fraser -- Managing and governing health care organizations / Anthony R. Kovner and Christy Harris Lemak -- Health information technology / Nirav R. Shah -- The future of health care delivery and health policy / James R. Knickman and Anthony R. Kovner. Subjects: Delivery of Health Care--United States. Health Policy--United States. Health Services--United States. Quality of Health Care--United States. Notes: Editors' names reversed on the previous edition. Preceded by: Jonas & Kovner's health care delivery in the United States. Includes bibliographical references and index.

Lean thinking for healthcare LCCN: 2013947473 Main title: Lean thinking for healthcare / Nilmini Wickramasinghe with Latif Al-Hakim, Chris Gonzalez, Joseph Tan, editors. Published/Produced: New York: Springer, [2014] ©2014 Description: xxxii, 645 pages: illustrations; 24 cm. ISBN: 9781461480358 (alk. paper) 1461480353 (alk. paper) LC classification: RA971 .L3668 2014 Related names: Wickramasinghe, Nilmini, author, editor. Al-Hakim, Latif, 1946- editor. Gonzalez, Chris, editor. Tan, Joseph K. H., editor. Summary: A growing, aging population; the rise to epidemic proportions of various chronic diseases; competing, often overlapping medical technologies; and of course, skyrocketing costs compounded by waste and inefficiency - these are just a few of the multifarious challenges currently facing healthcare delivery. An unexpected source of solutions is being imported from the manufacturing sector: lean thinking. "Lean Principles for Healthcare" presents a conceptual framework, management principles, and practical tools for professionals tasked with designing and implementing modern, streamlined healthcare systems or overhauling faulty ones. Focusing on core components such as knowledge management, e-health, patient-centeredness, and collaborative care, chapters illustrate lean concepts in action across specialties (as diverse as nursing, urology, and emergency care) and around the globe. Extended case examples show health systems responding to consumer needs and provider realities with equal efficiency and effectiveness, and improved quality and patient outcomes. Further, contributors tackle the gamut of technological, medical, cultural, and business issues -- Source other than Library of Congress. Contents: Pt. I. Key concepts, tools and techniques -- pt. II. Applications of lean thinking around the healthcare world -- pt. III. Macro issues -- pt. IV. Micro issues -- pt. V. Case studies. Subjects: Health services administration. Medical informatics--Management. Medical innovations--Management. Health Services Administration--economics. Quality of Health Care--economics. Efficiency, Organizational. Health Care Costs. Health Care Sector--organization & administration. Medical Informatics--economics. Notes: Includes bibliographical references and index. Series: Healthcare delivery in the information age Healthcare delivery in the information age.

Medical care economic risk: measuring financial vulnerability from spending on medical care LCCN: 2012554770 Corporate name: Panel on Measuring Medical Care Risk in Conjunction with the New Supplemental Income Poverty Measure. Main title: Medical care economic risk: measuring financial vulnerability from spending on medical care / Panel on Measuring Medical Care Risk in Conjunction with the New Supplemental Income Poverty Measure; Michael J. O'Grady and Gooloo S. Wunderlich, editors; Committee on National Statistics, Division of Behavioral and Social Sciences and Education and Board on Health Care Services; Institute of Medicine; National Research Council and Institute of

Medicine of the National Academies. Published/Produced: Washington, D.C.: National Academies Press, [2012] ©2012 Description: xvi, 293 pages: illustrations; 23 cm Links: National Academies Press http://www.nap.edu/catalog.php ?record_id=13525 ISBN: 9780309266048 (pbk.) 0309266041 (pbk.) LC classification: RA410 .P36 2012 Related names: O'Grady, Michael J. (Health policy expert), editor. Wunderlich, Gooloo S., editor. Summary: "The United States has seen major advances in medical care during the past decades, but access to care at an affordable cost is not universal. Many Americans lack health care insurance of any kind, and many others with insurance are nonetheless exposed to financial risk because of high premiums, deductibles, co-pays, limits on insurance payments, and uncovered services. One might expect that the U.S. poverty measure would capture these financial effects and trends in them over time. Yet the current official poverty measure developed in the early 1960s does not take into account significant increases and variations in medical care costs, insurance coverage, out-of-pocket spending, and the financial burden imposed on families and individuals. Although medical costs consume a growing share of family and national income and studies regularly document high rates of medical financial stress and debt, the current poverty measure does not capture the consequences for families' economic security or their income available for other basic needs. In 1995, a panel of the National Research Council (NRC) recommended a new poverty measure, which compares families' disposable income to poverty thresholds based on current spending for food, clothing, shelter, utilities, and a little more. The panel's recommendations stimulated extensive collaborative research involving several government agencies on experimental poverty measures that led to a new research Supplemental Poverty Measure (SPM), which the U.S. Census Bureau first published in November 2011 and will update annually. Analyses of the effects of including and excluding certain factors from the new SPM showed that, were it not for the cost that families incurred for premiums and other medical expenses not covered by health insurance, 10 million fewer people would have been poor according to the SPM. The implementation of the patient Protection and Affordable Care Act (ACA) provides a strong impetus to think rigorously about ways to measure medical care economic burden and risk, which is the basis for Medical Care Economic Risk. As new policies - whether part of the ACA or other policies - are implemented that seek to expand and improve health insurance coverage and to protect against the high costs of medical care relative to income, such measures will be important to assess the effects of policy changes in both the short and long term on the extent of financial burden and risk for the population, which are explained in this report"--Publisher's description. Contents: Review and recommendations (Introduction -- Concepts of medical care economic burden and risk -- Concepts of resources -- Measures of medical care economic risk and recommended approach -- Data sources -- Implementing measures of medical care economic burden and risk) -- Resources for the study: developing a measure of medical care economic risk- workshop summary (Introduction -- Context for the workshop -- Measuring medical care economic risk -- Issues in the development of thresholds -- issues in defining resources -- Implementation issues -- Recap of issues and next steps) -- Resources for the study: background papers (Conceptual framework for measuring medical care economic risk -- Incorporating data on assets into measures of financial burdens of health -- An assessment of data sources for measuring medical care economic risk). Subjects: Medical care, Cost of--Risk assessment--United States. Health Care Costs--United States. Health Expenditures--United States. Delivery of Health Care--economics--United States. Risk Assessment--United States. Universal Coverage--economics--United States. Notes: Includes bibliographical references. Additional formats: Also available online.

Neurodegeneration: exploring commonalities across diseases: workshop summary LCCN: 2014395561 Meeting name: Neurodegeneration: Opportunities for Collaboration Across Disease-Specific Research and Development Communities (Workshop), (2012: Washington, D.C.) Main title: Neurodegeneration: exploring commonalities across diseases: workshop summary / Miriam Davis and Clare Stroud, rapporteurs; Forum on Neuroscience and Nervous System Disorders, Board on Health Sciences Policy, Institute of Medicine of the National Academies. Published/Produced: Washington, D.C.: National Academies Press, [2013] ©2013 Description: xi, 93 pages: illustrations (chiefly color); 24 cm Links: National Academies Press http://www.nap.edu/catalog.php?record_id=18341 ISBN: 9780309285674 0309285674 LC classification: R856.A2 N475 2013 Related names: Davis, Miriam (Medical writer), author. Stroud, Clare, author. Institute of Medicine (U.S.). Forum on Neuroscience and Nervous System Disorders, sponsoring body. Summary: "Neurodegeneration: Exploring Commonalities Across Diseases is the summary of a workshop hosted by the Institute of Medicine's (IOM's) Forum on Neuroscience and Nervous System Disorders in Spring 2012 to explore commonalities across neurodegenerative diseases such as Alzheimer's disease, Parkinson's disease, amyotrophic lateral sclerosis (ALS), and frontotemporal dementia (FTD). Participants from academia; pharmaceutical and biotechnology industries; government agencies such as the National Institutes of Health and the U.S. Department of Veterans Affairs (VA); patient advocacy groups; and private foundations presented and identified potential opportunities for collaboration across the respective research and development communities. This report identifies and discusses commonalities related to genetic and cellular mechanisms, identifies areas of fundamental science needed to facilitate therapeutics development, and explores areas of potential collaboration among the respective research communities. Neurodegenerative diseases, such as Alzheimer's disease, Parkinson's disease, ALS, and FTD, are becoming increasingly prevalent in the United States due to an aging population. Implications are grave for quality of life and health care costs. Research on neurodegenerative diseases has expanded greatly over the past four decades. Nevertheless, fundamental questions remain about the biology of these diseases, and further insights into the mechanisms of these diseases would help to inform the development of effective means to prevent and to efficiently treat them. Recent findings have revealed certain commonalities in genetic and cellular mechanisms across neurodegenerative diseases. These findings suggest that it might be valuable - at least in some cases - to change the traditional way of studying these diseases by no longer seeing each as an independent entity, but rather as clinical variants of common cellular and molecular biological defects. This approach could help enhance basic scientific understanding of neurodegenerative disease, and could help with the development of biomarkers and new therapeutics." Contents: Introduction -- Rationale for exploring commonalities across neurodegenerative diseases -- Protein aggregation -- Transmissibility -- Mitochondrial pathology -- Errors in RNA -- Closing remarks. Subjects: Nervous system--Degeneration--Congresses. Biology--Research--Congresses. Neurodegenerative Diseases--Congresses. Biomedical Research--Congresses. Research Design--Congresses. Notes: Includes bibliographical references (pages 69-76). Additional formats: Online version: Neurodegeneration: Opportunities for Collaboration Across Disease-Specific Research and Development Communities (Workshop), (2012: Washington, D.C.). Neurodegeneration: exploring commonalities across diseases: workshop summary. Washington, D.C.: National Academies Press, 2013 (OCoLC)866949752

Pharmaphobia: how the conflict of interest myth undermines American medical innovation LCCN: 2014042834 Personal name: Stossel, Thomas P., author. Main title: Pharmaphobia: how the conflict of interest myth undermines American medical innovation / Thomas P. Stossel. Published/Produced: Lanham: Rowman & Littlefield, [2015] Description: p.; cm. ISBN: 9781442244627 (cloth: alk. paper) LC classification: RA418.3.U6 Contents: The stakes -- A practitioner's history of medical innovation -- Enter the conflict-of-interest mania -- The mania mongers -- Abusing evidence -- Bad policy process -- Flawed and damaging policies -- Misunderstanding innovation --

Economic illiteracy -- Misplaced criticism of incremental innovation -- Rushing to judgment with product safety alarms -- Demonizing marketing is false advertising -- The 'gift' smoke screen -- The lawyers' ball -- The price we pay -- What is to be done?. Subjects: Delivery of Health Care--United States. Inventions--United States. Conflict of Interest--United States. Consumer Product Safety--United States. Health Care Costs--United States. Marketing of Health Services--United States. Notes: Includes bibliographical references and index.

Quality care, affordable care: how physicians can reduce variation and lower healthcare costs
LCCN: 2013444974 Personal name: Shapiro, Lawrence, author. Main title: Quality care, affordable care: how physicians can reduce variation and lower healthcare costs / Lawrence Shapiro, MD. Published/Produced: Phoenix, Maryland: Greenbranch Publishing, [2014] Description: xviii, 183 pages: illustrations, portrait; 23 cm ISBN: 9780991013500 (pbk.) 0991013506 (pbk.) LC classification: RA410.5 .S4 2014 Subjects: Physician's Practice Patterns--economics--United States. Health Care Costs--United States. Health Care Reform--United States. Physician's Role--United States. Quality of Health Care--economics--United States. Notes: Includes bibliographical references (pages 171-173) and index.

Redefining health care systems
LCCN: 2015013738 Personal name: Brook, Robert H. (Robert Henry), 1943- , author, editor. Main title: Redefining health care systems / Robert H. Brook. Published/Produced: Santa Monica, CA: RAND, [2015] Description: p.; cm. ISBN: 9780833090409 (pbk.: alk. paper) LC classification: RA398.A3 Related titles: JAMA. Contents: Health status can be measured -- Free care increases health service use but does not improve health -- Patient copayments strongly influence health care use -- How physicians are paid influences how they practice -- Quality of care can be measured -- Quality of care varies -- The appropriateness of care can be determined -- Geography is a strong predictor of health service use -- Depression, a leading cause of morbidity, is poorly detected and poorly treated --

Physicians and patients need tools to support decisionmaking -- Person's waste is another's income -- Social factors are powerful determinants of health -- Science and technology will increase health care costs -- How health services research can fix the health care system -- Stories -- Story one -- Story two -- Story three -- Story four -- Story five -- Story six -- Story seven -- Story eight. Subjects: Delivery of Health Care--organization & administration--United States. Health Status--United States. Health Services Research--United States. Notes: "The third section of the book comprises a series of short commentaries on specific issues, originally published in JAMA between March 2009 and March 2012." Includes bibliographical references. Additional formats: Online version: Brook, Robert H. (Robert Henry), 1943- , author, editor. Redefining health care systems Santa Monica, CA: RAND, [2015] 9780833090416 (DLC) 2015014088

Redefining healthcare philanthropy LCCN: 2014940647 Main title: Redefining healthcare philanthropy / editor, Betsy Chapin Taylor; foreword by William McGinly. Published/Produced: Falls Church, VA: Association for Healthcare Philanthropy, 2014 ©2014 Description: xv, 217 pages: illustrations; 23 cm ISBN: 9780985321147 LC classification: RA410.5 .R433 2014 Related names: Chapin, Betsy Taylor, editor. Association for Healthcare Philanthropy (U.S.), publisher. Subjects: Fund raising. Medical care. Fund Raising. Health Care Costs. Fund raising. Medical care. Notes: Includes bibliographiical references.

Steering clear: how to avoid a debt crisis and secure our economic future LCCN: 2014038638 Personal name: Peterson, Peter G. Main title: Steering clear: how to avoid a debt crisis and secure our economic future / Peter G. Peterson. Published/Produced: New York, New York: Portfolio/Penguin, 2015. Description: x, 192 pages: color illustrations, charts; 24 cm Links: Cover image ftp://ppftpuser:welcome@ftp01.penguingroup.com/Booksellers and Media/Covers/2008_2009_New_Covers/9781591847809.jpg ISBN: 9781591847809 (hardback) LC classification: HC106.83 .P48 2015 Summary: " "Despite clear danger and explicit warnings, the United

States of America-distracted by short-term challenges and its own political dysfunction-is steaming toward its own collision, one with long-term debt." Philanthropist, businessman, and former secretary of commerce Peter G. Peterson argues that we can no longer ignore the long-term debt challenges facing our country, because our economic future depends on it. The gross federal debt now exceeds $17 trillion and it is expected to rise rapidly in the decades to come. If the growing gap between projected spending and revenues continues to widen, our federal debt is projected to soar to the highest levels in our nation's history-more than four times its average over the past forty years. This growing debt and the associated interest costs divert resources away from important public and private investments that are critical to our global competitiveness, threatening our future economy. Peterson has made it his life's work to bring awareness to America's key economic and fiscal challenges. He makes clear that if we continue to ignore America's long-term debt, we will diminish economic opportunities for future generations, weaken our ability to protect the most vulnerable, and undermine the competitive strength of our businesses globally. The drama-filled, economically damaging budget battles of the last few years have focused almost entirely on the short term-putting aside the more difficult, but much more important, long-term issues. Peterson offers nonpartisan analysis of our economic challenges and a robust set of options for solving our long-term debt problems. He looks at the impact of aging baby boomers, growing healthcare costs, outdated military spending, a flawed tax code, and our divided political system. And he offers hopeful, durable, and achievable solutions for improving our fiscal outlook through a mix of progrowth reform options that would reduce government spending and increase revenue, and could be phased in gradually in the years to come. There's still time to restore the United States as a land of opportunity. Peterson's diagnosis and recommendations can help us confront our fiscal reality, address our long-term debt, and steer the country safely toward a more secure and dynamic economic future"-- Provided by publisher. "Philanthropist, businessman, and former

Secretary of Commerce Peter G. Peterson argues that America must address its long-term debt in order to build a strong economy, today and in the future. If we continue to ignore America's unsustainable fiscal challenges, we are steering our country towards a collision with long-term debt that will diminish economic opportunities for the next generation, weaken our ability to protect vulnerable people, and undermine the competitive strength of our businesses in a vastly more global and technological world. The gross federal debt now exceeds $17 trillion, and it is projected to soar in coming decades, diverting resources from the critical private and public investments we need to make in education, R&D, and infrastructure to secure our economic future and Americans' well-being. Yet Washington is gridlocked, risking a crippled economy for our children and grandchildren. Peterson offers a non-partisan analysis of our dilemma and a robust set of options for solving our long-term debt problem. He looks at the impact of aging baby boomers, growing health care costs, outdated military spending, our flawed tax code, and our divided political system. And he shows how we can improve our fiscal outlook through a mix of pro-growth reforms that would reduce government spending and increase revenue, which could be phased in gradually in the years to come once our economy has recovered"-- Provided by publisher. Subjects: Deficit financing--United States. Debt--United States. Business & Economics / Economic Conditions. Business & Economics / Government & Business. United States--Economic conditions--21st century. United States--Economic policy--21st century. Notes: Includes index.

The Affordable Care Act LCCN: 2014021942 Main title: The Affordable Care Act / Tamara Thompson, Book Editor. Published/Produced: Farmington Hills, Mich.: Greenhaven Press, [2015] Description: 128 pages; 24 cm. ISBN: 9780737771497 (hbk.) 0737771496 (hbk.) 9780737771503 (pbk.) 073777150X (pbk.) LC classification: KF3605.A328201 A2 2015a Related names: Thompson, Tamara, editor. Contents: ObamaCare: The plan is to transition to "single-payer" socialized medicine / William F. Jasper -- The Affordable Care

Act is not socialized medicine / Victor Pena -- The Affordable Care Act falls short of health care as a human right / Anja Rudiger -- Millions of poor are left uncovered by health law / Sabrina Tavernise and Robert Gebeloff -- Obamacare: What if not enough young, healthy people enroll? / Linda Feldmann -- The Affordable Care Act will benefit rich and poor alike / Froma Harrop -- The Affordable Care Act will help contain health-care costs / Stephen Zuckerman and John Holahan -- Insurance racket / Andrew Stiles -- The Affordable Care Act will hurt the US economy / Sara Marie Brenner -- The Affordable Care Act should be repealed / The Heritage Foundation -- Most Americans oppose repealing the Affordable Care Act / Ronald Brownstein -- Calling the Affordable Care Act "Obamacare" undermines reform / Mugambi Jouet -- Misallocation of Obamacare showcases modern race bias / The Gazette -- Botched ACA rollout could taint President Obama's legacy / Cleveland Plain Dealer -- Despite a botched rollout, the health-care law is worth it / Alan S. Blinder. Subjects: United States. Patient Protection and Affordable Care Act. Health insurance--Law and legislation--United States. Health care reform--United States. Notes: Includes bibliographical references (pages 113-122) and index. Series: At issue

The Affordable Care Act: a missed opportunity, a better way forward LCCN: 2013007688 Personal name: Faguet, Guy B. Main title: The Affordable Care Act: a missed opportunity, a better way forward / Guy B. Faguet. Published/Created: New York: Algora Pub., c2013. Description: x, 236 p.; 23 cm. ISBN: 9780875869759 (soft cover: alk. paper) 9780875869766 (hard cover: alk. paper) 9780875869773 (ebook) LC classification: RA971.3 .F34 2013 Contents: Historical overview -- Root causes of the spiraling healthcare costs -- Cost control initiatives -- The politics and the money behind the bill -- Outline of the Affordable Care Act -- The U.S. healthcare system: a brief outline -- Foreign and domestic health models we can learn from -- An equitable and affordable universal health system. Subjects: United States. Patient Protection and Affordable Care Act. National Health Insurance, United States--United States. Health Care

Costs--United States. Health Care Reform--United States. Insurance, Health--economics--United States. Notes: Includes bibliographical references and index.

The cost disease: why computers get cheaper and health care doesn't LCCN: 2012938269 Personal name: Baumol, William J. Main title: The cost disease: why computers get cheaper and health care doesn't / William J. Baumol; with contributions by David de Ferranti ... [et al.]. Published/Created: New Haven: Yale University Press, c2012. Description: xxi, 249 p.: ill.; 22 cm. ISBN: 9780300179286 (hbk.) 0300179286 (hbk.) LC classification: RA410.53 .B386 2012 Related names: De Ferranti, David M. Contents: Part I: The survivable cost disease. Why health-care costs keep rising; What causes the cost disease, and will it persist?; The future has arrived; Yes, we can afford it; Dark sides of the disease: terrorism and environmental destruction; Common misunderstandings of the cost disease: cost versus quality and financial versus "physical" output measures; The cost disease and global health -- Part 2: Technical aspects of the cost disease. Hybrid industries and the cost disease; Productivity growth, employment allocation, and the special case of business services -- Part 3: Opportunities for cutting health-care costs. Business services in health care; Yes, we can cut health-care costs even if we cannot reduce their growth rate -- Conclusions: Where are we headed and what should we do? Subjects: Medical care, Cost of--United States. Health Care Costs--United States. Cost of Illness--United States. Notes: Includes bibliographical references (p. 207-235) and index.

The doctor's book of natural health remedies: unlock the power of alternative healing and find your path back to health LCCN: 2012278113 Personal name: Moline, Peg. Main title: The doctor's book of natural health remedies: unlock the power of alternative healing and find your path back to health / Peg Moline and the editors of Natural Health. Published/Produced: New York: Galvanized Books, a division of Galvanized Brands, LLC, [2014] Description: xv, 480 pages: illustrations; 24 cm ISBN: 9780989594080 (pbk.) 0989594084 (pbk.) LC classification: RZ440 .M65 2014 Variant title: Pre-publication title was given as: Complete book of natural health remedies: 1001 new answers from the world of alternative medicine Portion of title: Book of natural health remedies Natural health remedies Related names: Natural Health (Publisher) Summary: "With health care costs rising, insurance systems in flux, doctors and hospitals overwhelmed, the only person who can really take charge of your health and the health of your family is you. This is your guide. For more than 40 years, Natural Health has been the leading authority on holistic, alternative, and natural healing. Now, for the first time ever, all that science-based, expert-driven, research-intensive information has been distilled into one must-have, authoritative guide to healing the self. In these pages, you'll find stunning new research, unparalleled expert advice, how-to health guides, and a scientific, myth-debunking approach to natural remedies. Search for your symptoms. Find your cure. The power is yours. A clean life for you--and your family--starts now"-- from publisher's web site. Subjects: Naturopathy--Popular works. Alternative medicine--Popular works. Self-care, Health. Notes: Includes index.

The grassroots health care revolution: how companies across America are dramatically cutting their health care costs while improving care LCCN: 2013041457 Personal name: Torinus, John, Jr., author. Main title: The grassroots health care revolution: how companies across America are dramatically cutting their health care costs while improving care / John Torinus Jr. Published/Produced: Dallas, Texas: BenBella Books, Inc., [2014] Description: xiv, 209 pages; 22 cm. ISBN: 9781939529725 (trade cloth: alk. paper) LC classification: RA412.3 .T67 2014 Summary: "When exploding health care costs threatened Serigraphs solvency, the CEO went outside the box to find a solution. John Torinus Jr. applied innovative, cutting-edge strategies to cut his health care expenses well below the national average while improving his employees care. Now, across America, leading companies are following Serigraphs example. There is a revolution brewing. A revolution that will dramatically lower health costs nationwide. John Torinus Jr., author of The Company That Solved Health Care, the eye-opening book detailing one company's game-changing health care program, now presents The Grassroots Health Care Revolution. Featuring examples and interviews with the business leaders who are at the forefront of these innovations, The Grassroots Health Care Revolution is a game plan for improving workforce health and radically lowering health costs. Torinus avoids the politics of health care to focus on what businesses can actually control. He shows how pioneering corporations have engaged their employees to tame the hyper-inflation that has plagued the health care industry for decades. Executives in leading companies are deploying management disciplines and marketplace principles to invent a better business model for health care. These companies are bending the curve, growing profits and improving the health of their employees. Learn how you and your business can join the revolution"--Provided by publisher. Contents: Go or no-go under Obamacare? -- Private payers forge disruptive new business model -- Three-year game plan can flatline company health costs -- Self-insurance: companies keep their health savings -- Consumer-driven: companies engage employees -- Transparency: entrepreneurs shine light on prices, Quality -- Centers of value: companies move business -- Restructured pricing: companies demand better models -- On-site clinics: companies take over primary care -- Chronic diseases: companies go where the money goes -- Health as asset: companies come to new understanding -- Other payers join the marketplace revolution -- Employees, employers, nation: win-win-win. Subjects: Health Benefit Plans, Employee--economics--United States. Costs and Cost Analysis--economics--United States. Health Care Reform--economics--United States. National Health Insurance, United States--economics--United States. Notes: Includes bibliographical references.

The lean prescription: powerful medicine for our ailing healthcare system LCCN: 2014034111 Personal name: Gabow, Patricia A., author. Main title: The lean prescription: powerful medicine for our ailing healthcare system / Patricia A. Gabow, MD, MACP, Philip L. Goodman. Published/Produced: Boca Raton: CRC Press, Taylor & Francis Group, [2015] ©2015 Description: xxii, 161 pages: illustrations; 24 cm. ISBN:

9781482246384 (hardback: acid-free paper) 1482246384 (hardback: acid-free paper) LC classification: RA401.A3 G328 2015 Related names: Goodman, Philip L., author. Summary: "This book is written by a seasoned physician, teacher, and scientist who was the CEO of a large integrated system for 20 years. It is a complete how-to book on implementing a Lean transformation in a health care system that includes not only a hospital but also HMO, CHC, and paramedics. Providing an accessible explanation of the Lean philosophy and tools, the book outlines a detailed approach to Lean implementation. It includes exercises and examples of Lean applications that go beyond the hospital to include CHC, paramedics, and poison centers"--Provided by publisher. Subjects: Delivery of Health Care--economics--United States. Cost Savings--methods--United States. Health Care Costs--United States. Quality of Health Care--United States. Notes: Includes bibliographical references (pages 153-155) and index. Series: A Productivity Press book

The Malthusian century LCCN: 2013045181 Main title: The Malthusian century / Charles T. Stewart, Jr. Published/Produced: New York: Nova Publishers, 2014. ©2014 Description: vi, 169 pages; 24 cm ISBN: 9781629486673 (hardcover) 1629486671 (hardcover) LC classification: HB75 .M246 2014 Related names: Stewart, Charles T., 1922- Contents: Introduction -- The industrial revolution is over -- Alternative energy: geography and arithmetic -- Climate change and common sense -- Ecophilia -- A place to live -- Savings, investment and salvation -- College: investment, insurance, or lottery ticket? -- Medical education and health care costs -- Consumerism -- Depression in the household economy -- Obsolescence and employment: are more jobs necessary? -- Inequality -- Egalitarianism or life as a lottery -- Living on $3,650 a year in the USA -- When solutions are the problem -- No good deed goes unpunished -- Is democracy a Ponzi scheme? -- Democracy and religion -- National identity, national goals -- Population bust? -- Shrinking cities -- The right to emigrate -- Who am I? -- Solitude -- On living too long -- In defense of marriage -- Restructuring society -- Chinese checkers -- The war of words --

Wars of the 21st century -- Past and future history -- Farewell to affluence. Subjects: Malthus, T. R. (Thomas Robert), 1766-1834. Economics--History. Overpopulation--History. Environmentalism--History. Series: Social issues, justice and status

The weight of the nation: surprising lessons about diets, food, and fat from the extraordinary HBO documentary series LCCN: 2012001376 Personal name: Hoffman, John. Main title: The weight of the nation: surprising lessons about diets, food, and fat from the extraordinary HBO documentary series / John Hoffman and Judith A. Salerno, with Alexandra Moss; foreword by Kelly D. Brownell; afterword by Harvey V. Fineberg. Edition: 1st ed. Published/Created: New York: St. Martin's Press, 2012. Description: xiii, 206 p.; 25 cm. ISBN: 9781250014733 (hardback) 9781250014740 (e-book) LC classification: RC628 .H64 2012 Related names: Salerno, Judith A., 1959- Brownell, Kelly D. Fineberg, Harvey V. Summary: “Readers know America is getting fatter but might not know that 75% of us may be overweight or obese by 2018, that children are at risk for obesity and diabetes as never before, or that obesity is the number one cause of the rise in our nation's health care costs. They might also believe, like many Americans, that obesity results from a lack of self-control. But people today work harder and take better care of their health than ever before. So how could three-quarters of us somehow suddenly lack willpower when it comes to eating right and exercising? HBO, together with the Institute of Medicine of the National Academies, has gathered the nation's foremost experts to explain how we got here and how we can overcome the forces that drive us to eat too much and move too little. --Is exercise enough to help most people maintain an ideal weight? --Could weighing too much during pregnancy set my child up for a lifetime of poor health? --Do “fat kids” ever grow out of it? --How do lack of sleep and too much stress contribute to weight gain? --Why can I eat the same amount as my friend, but I gain weight and she never does? HBO's four-part documentary series premieres in May 2012 and examines the serious health consequences of obesity, shows viewers how to help themselves and their children live healthier lives, looks at the obesity epidemic from every angle, and explores the growing epidemic of childhood obesity"-- Provided by publisher. Subjects: Obesity--United States. Food habits--United States. Public health--United States. Health & Fitness / Weight Loss.

U.S. health policy and politics: a documentary history LCCN: 2011019493 Personal name: Hillstrom, Kevin, 1963- Main title: U.S. health policy and politics: a documentary history / Kevin Hillstrom. Published/Created: Washington, DC: CQ Press, c2012. Description: xxiii, 717 p.; 26 cm. ISBN: 9781608710263 (alk. paper) LC classification: RA395.A3 H555 2012 Contents: Health care and medical practice in the new world, 1600-1800 -- Health care and regulation in antebellum America, 1800-1860 -- The professionalization of American medicine, 1860-1890 -- Health care in the progressive era, 1890-1920 -- The struggle over health insurance between the wars, 1920-1940 -- Partisan jousting over health care in the postwar era, 1940-1960 -- Medicare changes the health care landscape, 1960-1980 -- Restraining health care costs in the age of Reagan, 1980-1990 -- The Clinton health plan and scorched-earth politics, 1990-2000 -- Controversial policy prescriptions for American health care, 2000-2010. Subjects: Medical policy--United States--History. Medical laws and legislation--United States--History. Health Policy--history--United States. Delivery of Health Care--history--United States. Health Policy--legislation & jurisprudence--United States. History, Modern 1601---United States. Politics--United States. Notes: Includes bibliographical references (p. 689-692) and index.

Understanding health care reform: bridging the gap between myth and reality LCCN: 2011044916 Personal name: Feldman, Arthur M. (Arthur Michael), 1949- Main title: Understanding health care reform: bridging the gap between myth and reality / Arthur M. Feldman. Published/Created: Boca Raton: Taylor & Francis, c2012. Description: xxiv, 198 p.; 24 cm. ISBN: 9781439879481 (hardback: alk. paper) LC classification: RA395.A3 F45 2012 Summary: "This book provides an understanding of the strengths and weaknesses of the health care reform legislation. It explains how doctors, patients, and families can determine the success or failure of the legislation over time. The author describes how to ensure that this landmark legislation succeeds in achieving its goals and proposes an accounting of steps that elected representatives can take in order to improve the bill. The text cuts through the political rhetoric and focuses on the core issue: what we need to do to preserve our ability to provide the best possible care for our patients and to fulfill our societal mission of providing care for our citizens independent of their financial means"--Provided by publisher. Incomplete contents: Reforming the private insurance industry -- How will health care reform affect the Medicare and Medicaid populations? -- Can we lower health care costs by eliminating waste? -- The role of disease prevention in health care reform -- How will health care reform affect the medically under-served and the safety net hospitals that care for them? -- How can we improve the quality of care in the U.S.? -- Will there be enough doctors to care for 35 million new patients? -- Can research guide us to improved care at lower costs? -- How will health care reform change the way we practice medicine? -- Will we ever see tort reform in the U.S.? Subjects: United States. Patient Protection and Affordable Care Act. Health Care Reform--legislation & jurisprudence--United States. Insurance, Health--legislation & jurisprudence--United States. Medically Uninsured--legislation & jurisprudence--United States. Notes: Includes bibliographical references and index.

Unintimidated: a governor's story and a nation's challenge LCCN: 2013036131 Personal name: Walker, Scott (Scott Kevin), 1967- Main title: Unintimidated: a governor's story and a nation's challenge / Scott Walker with Marc Thiessen. Published/Produced: New York: Sentinel, [2013] Description: x, 278 pages: illustrations; 24 cm ISBN: 9781595231079 (hardback) LC classification: F586.42.W35 A3 2013 Related names: Thiessen, Marc A. Summary: "A controversial governor recounts his fight to reform his state and issues a call to action for the whole country In 2010, Scott Walker was elected governor of Wisconsin with a mandate to improve its economy and restore fiscal responsibility. With the state facing a $3.6 billion budget deficit, he proposed a series of reforms to limit the collective bargaining power of public employee unions, which was costing taxpayers billions in pension and health care costs. The reaction was swift and severe. Angry protesters gathered outside the capitol, teacher unions accused him of sabotaging education, and the media descended on Wisconsin to make it a national controversy. Soon, liberals nationwide were denouncing Governor Walker. He stood his ground despite relentless political and personal attacks with the help of supporters across the country who hailed him for having the courage to drive real change. In June 2012, he won a special recall election with a higher share of the vote than he had for his original election, becoming the first governor in the country to survive a recall election. In this book, Governor Walker shows how his commitment to limited but effective government paid off. During his tenure Wisconsin has saved more than $1 billion, property taxes have gone down for the first time in twelve years, and the deficit was turned into a surplus. He also shows what his experiences can teach defenders of liberty across the country about standing up to the special interests that favor the status quo"-- Provided by publisher. Subjects: Walker, Scott (Scott Kevin), 1967- Governors--Wisconsin--Biography. Political Science / Political Ideologies / Conservatism & Liberalism. Political Science / Government / State & Provincial. Political Science / General. Wisconsin--Politics and government--1951- Notes: Includes bibliographical references and index.

Unlocking the mystery of health care planning for retirement LCCN: 2012288942 Personal name: Sullivan, James Main title: Unlocking the mystery of health care planning for retirement / James Sullivan. Published/Created: New York: American Institute of Certified Public Accountants, c2012 Description: x, 86 p.; 25 cm. ISBN: 9781937350581 1937350584 LC classification: HQ1062 .S82 2012 Related names: American Institute of Certified Public Accountants. Summary: "This guide was designed by CPAs for CPAs... to provide an overview of the resources available to clients as they consider how they will pay for their health care costs during retirement. Although many resources are available that provide Medicare facts or advice... few are oriented toward professionals seeking to offer guidance to clients... This guide is meant to be a practical resource that blends information and planning guidance..." -- From publisher. Contents: Ch. 1 The scope of the problem and extent of the opportunity -- Ch. 2 An overview of Medicare -- Ch. 3 Traditional Medicare enrollment -- Ch. 4 Traditional Medicare covered health expenses -- Ch. 5 Traditional Medicare payment and premium structure -- Ch. 6 Medicare supplement policies -- Ch. 7 Medicare Part D prescription drug coverage -- Ch. 8 Medicare advantage plans -- Ch. 9 Medicare: special tax considerations -- Ch. 10 Long-term care -- Appendix: The client interview. Subjects: Retirement--Planning. Baby boom generation--Health aspects. Baby boom generation--Finance, Personal--Planning. Older people--Health aspects. Aging--Economic aspects. Medicare. Long-term care of the sick.

INDEX

#

21st century, 79, 101, 110, 116

A

abuse, 99, 100
access, 75, 81, 84, 89, 90, 96, 98, 103
accessibility, 75, 83, 97
accommodation, 94
accounting, 92, 118
acid, 78, 115
adjustment, 30, 54, 79
advancement, 79
advocacy, 105
aetiology, 93
affluence, 116
Africa, 96
age, 11, 12, 19, 20, 21, 23, 24, 26, 68, 76, 92, 102, 117
agencies, 103, 105
aggregation, 106
aging population, 101, 105
aging society, 77
alcohol dependence, 29
algorithm, 24, 25
ALS, 105
alternative medicine, 113
American Recovery and Reinvestment Act, 85
amyotrophic lateral sclerosis, 105
anastomosis, 52, 68, 70, 73
anemia, 4
angiography, 28
antitrust, 95
anxiety, 5
appendectomy, 50
arithmetic, 115
Armenia, 97
assessment, 3, 50, 82, 93, 104
assets, 104
attitudes, 20
authority, 113
awareness, 109

B

baby boomers, 109
bargaining, 119
barriers, 78
base, 82, 89
basic needs, 103
Bayesian estimation, 28
bending, 114
benefits, 18, 26, 55, 77, 84, 91
benign, 70
bias, 79, 111
biomarkers, 106
biotechnology, 105
blends, 120

blood, 22, 34, 35, 36, 54, 69
blood transfusion, 54
blueprint, 98
Brazil, 52, 96
budget allocation, 26
Budget Committee, 80
budget deficit, 118
Bulgaria, 97
business model, 114
businesses, 109, 114

C

cancer, 5, 14, 18, 20, 21, 22, 26, 27, 30, 50, 51, 57, 70, 71, 72, 89
cancer care, 26, 89
care model, 96
caregivers, 76
case examples, 102
case studies, 21, 90, 99, 100
causation, 93
CD-ROM, 90
census, 76, 103
cervical cancer, 71, 72
cervix, 57
challenges, 28, 81, 89, 94, 95, 96, 101, 109
charities, 36, 69
chemotherapy, 18
childhood, 117
children, 81, 84, 110, 116
China, 96
cholecystectomy, 51
chronic diseases, 101
cities, 115
citizens, 78, 118
classes, 21
classification, 75, 76, 77, 78, 79, 80, 81, 82, 83, 84, 86, 87, 88, 90, 91, 92, 95, 96, 98, 99, 100, 101, 103, 105, 106, 107, 108, 110, 111, 112, 113, 115, 116, 117, 118, 119
clients, 119
Clinical Data Repository (CDR), viii, 2, 5, 18
clinical trials, 24, 28
clothing, 103
clustering, viii, 2, 26
coherence, 75
colectomy, 51
collaboration, 105
collective bargaining, 119
color, 77, 88, 90, 105, 108
colorectal cancer, 14, 31, 51
colorectal surgery, viii, 33, 50
commerce, 109
commercial, 2
common sense, 115
communication, 89
communities, 76, 81, 105
community, 85
comparative analysis, 72
compensation, 93
competition, viii, 33, 35, 49, 53, 55, 69
competitiveness, 109
compilation, 88
complexity, 7
complications, 35, 50, 52, 55, 70
composition, 23
computation, 13
computer, 79
conceptualization, 94
conflict, 106
conflict of interest, 106
congress, 29, 80, 89, 98, 102
consumption, 52
continuous data, 6, 9, 29
controversial, 118
controversies, 77, 94
conversion rate, 36, 69
correlation(s), 8, 9, 10, 12, 13, 14, 15, 16, 17, 19, 22, 23, 34, 35, 36, 49, 56
cosmetic, 35, 55
cost, vii, viii, 1, 2, 3, 4, 5, 6, 7, 8, 9, 10, 12, 13, 14, 16, 17, 18, 20, 21, 22, 23, 24, 26, 27, 28, 29, 31, 33, 34, 35, 36, 37, 38, 39, 40, 41, 42, 43, 44, 45, 46, 47, 48, 49, 50, 51, 52, 53, 54, 55, 56, 57, 58, 59, 60, 61, 62, 63, 64, 65, 66, 67, 68, 69, 70, 71, 72, 73, 87, 91, 93, 96, 98, 103, 112
cost analysis, 51, 53, 69, 71, 73, 86, 114

cost effectiveness, 34, 73
cost minimization, 51
cost saving, 56, 91
criticism, 107
crowding out, 88
Cuba, 96
cure, 113
Czech Republic, 97

D

da Vinci surgical system, 51
danger, 108
data analysis, 69
data collection, 2
data set, 28, 79
database, 5, 50
decentralization, 98
decision makers, 6
defects, 106
deficit, 81, 119
degenerate, 24
dementia, 105
democracy, 115
demographic characteristics, 26
dependent variable, 6, 28, 30
depression, 5
depth, 56
depth perception, 56
destruction, 112
developed countries, 96
developing countries, 75
dexterity, viii, 34, 53, 54
diabetes, 22, 116
dialysis, 4, 15
diffusion, 17
directives, 77
disability, 76, 92
diseases, 17, 20, 26, 97, 104, 114
disorder, 22
disposable income, 103
distribution, 6, 7, 9, 10, 12, 24, 87
doctors, 4, 35, 113, 117
drugs, 4, 18

E

E85, 98
Eastern Europe, 97
economic fear, 78
economic growth, 81
economics, 5, 79, 80, 87, 88, 89, 90, 95, 102, 104, 107, 112, 114, 115
editors, 92, 101, 102, 112
education, 20, 88, 110, 115, 119
elderly population, 84
elders, 77
election, 119
emergency, 102
employees, 93, 113
employers, 80, 114
employment, 94, 112, 115
endogeneity, 21
end-stage renal disease, 21
energy, 115
enrollment, 17, 120
entrepreneurs, 114
environment, 23, 91
epidemic, 101, 117
epithelial ovarian cancer, 14
equipment, 34, 35, 36, 37, 38, 39, 40, 41, 42, 43, 44, 45, 46, 47, 48, 49, 54, 55, 57, 58, 59, 60, 61, 62, 63, 64, 65, 66, 67, 68, 69
equity, 98
erythropoietin, 4, 15
ethical issues, 88
ethnicity, 76
Europe, 96, 97, 98
European Community, 54, 79
European Union, 75
evidence, viii, 17, 18, 24, 26, 28, 33, 34, 49, 50, 84, 86, 89, 93, 106
evolution, 33
exercise(s), 115, 116
expenditures, vii, 1, 4, 16, 17, 18, 20, 21, 27, 84, 90

F

families, viii, 2, 3, 5, 20, 21, 81, 84, 103, 117
family members, 5, 21, 69
fat, 116
FDA, 4
fear(s), 5, 78
federal mandate, 85
fibromyalgia, 93
financial, 5, 21, 26, 34, 36, 54, 56, 76, 78, 89, 102, 112, 118
financial condition, 54
financial crisis, 89
financial stability, 76
financial vulnerability, 102
fiscal year, 80
flexibility, 11
food, 103, 116
formation, 36, 95
foundations, 78, 105
France, 96
funding, 96

G

gastrectomy, 52
GDP, 88
general surgery, viii, 33, 34, 37, 49, 50, 51, 54
genetic screening, 77
geography, 115
gerontology, 78
good deed, 115
government spending, 109
governor, 118
grassroots, 113
Great Britain, 96
Greece, 33, 53, 54
gross domestic product, 1, 88
growth, vii, 1, 2, 18, 81, 88, 110, 112
growth rate, 112
guidance, 120
guidelines, 30, 93, 99, 100
gynecologic surgery, viii, 50, 53, 55, 70

H

hazards, 15, 16
HBV, 22
healing, 112
health, vii, 1, 2, 4, 5, 6, 10, 13, 14, 15, 17, 19, 20, 21, 22, 24, 25, 26, 27, 28, 29, 30, 31, 34, 35, 36, 54, 55, 56, 75, 76, 77, 78, 79, 80, 81, 83, 85, 86, 87, 88, 91, 92, 95, 96, 97, 98, 99, 100, 102, 103, 105, 107, 110, 111, 112, 113, 115, 116, 117, 119
health care, vii, 1, 2, 4, 20, 27, 28, 29, 30, 31, 34, 35, 36, 55, 56, 76, 77, 78, 79, 80, 81, 82, 83, 85, 87, 88, 91, 92, 95, 96, 97, 98, 99, 100, 103, 105, 107, 110, 111, 112, 113, 115, 116, 117, 119
health care costs, vii, 1, 27, 28, 76, 77, 78, 79, 80, 81, 82, 83, 84, 85, 86, 87, 88, 90, 91, 92, 95, 96, 97, 98, 100, 101, 102, 104, 105, 107, 108, 110, 112, 113, 115, 116, 117, 118, 119
health care expenditures, vii, 1
health care professionals, 100
health care system, 30, 34, 35, 36, 82, 83, 96, 97, 98, 107, 115
health condition, 21, 22
health expenditure, 14, 88
health insurance, 2, 29, 34, 54, 56, 84, 87, 99, 100, 104, 117
health outcomes, vii, 2, 14, 27, 82, 89
health plans, viii, 2
health promotion, 91
health risks, 91
health services, 83, 85, 91, 108
health status, 20, 24, 25, 84
healthcare cost, vii, 1, 107, 109, 111
heart failure, 3, 18, 30
hematocrit, 4
hepatopancreatic, viii, 33
heterogeneity, 4, 16, 18, 79
heteroscedasticity, 6, 9, 11, 24, 30
history, vii, 1, 2, 3, 85, 88, 106, 109, 116, 117

HIV, 84, 96
HIV/AIDS, 96
Hong Kong, 50
hospitalization, 4, 20, 22, 23, 36, 56
House, 80, 83, 85
House of Representatives, 80
human, 70, 93, 99, 100, 111
human resources, 93, 99, 100
human right, 111
Hungary, 97
hygiene, 91, 95
hysterectomy, 68, 69, 70, 71, 72

I

ideal, 116
identification, 82
identity, 115
illiteracy, 107
image(s), 91, 108
improvements, vii, 2, 90
incidence, 31, 93
income, 21, 77, 103, 108
India, 96
individuals, 4, 13, 20, 21, 22, 26, 78, 103
industrial revolution, 115
industries, 105, 112
industry, viii, 33, 49, 53, 69, 114, 118
inefficiency, 101
inequality, 96
infarction, 28
inferences, 97
inflation, 114
influenza, 21
information technology, 101
infrastructure, 86, 88, 110
inheritance, 77
injuries, 93
insecurity, 78
international competitiveness, 89
intervention, 19, 93
investment(s), 77, 81, 88, 115
IQR, 59, 60, 68
iron, 80
IRS, 92
issues, vii, 2, 4, 5, 21, 78, 83, 89, 92, 100, 102, 104, 108, 109, 116, 118

J

Jefferson, Thomas, 90

K

Korea, 51

L

labor force, 76, 78
landscape, 117
laparoscopic cholecystectomy, 51
laparoscopic colectomy, 51
laparoscopic surgery, 49, 51, 56, 71, 72
laparoscopy, 36, 48, 49, 50, 54, 55, 56, 69, 71, 72
laparotomy, 35, 36, 37, 38, 39, 40, 41, 42, 43, 44, 45, 46, 47, 48, 55, 57, 58, 59, 60, 61, 62, 63, 64, 65, 66, 67, 68, 69, 71, 72
laws, 117
lawyers, 107
lead, 6, 11, 14, 26, 78
leadership, 87
learning, 35, 49, 55, 70, 77, 86
legislation, 76, 85, 111, 117
liberty, 119
life course, 77
life expectancy, 29
lifetime, 14, 89, 116
light, 78, 114
linear function, 14
linear model, 6, 7, 27
living conditions, 82
longevity, 14
long-term debt, 109

M

Macedonia, 97

majority, 3, 20, 69
malaria, 96
management, 2, 3, 18, 35, 83, 93, 99, 100, 102, 114
mania, 106
manufacturing, 102
mapping, 24, 25
marital status, 68
marketing, 99, 100, 107
marketplace, 114
marriage, 20, 115
Maryland, 80, 107
mass, 3, 6, 15, 24
matrix, 6, 9, 10, 13, 14
matter, 85, 88
measurement, vii, 2, 82, 84, 85
media, 119
median, 18, 22, 37, 38, 39, 40, 41, 42, 43, 47, 48, 56, 57, 58, 59, 60, 63, 65, 67, 68
Medicaid, 2, 4, 5, 118
medical, vii, 1, 2, 3, 4, 5, 6, 7, 8, 9, 10, 11, 12, 13, 14, 15, 16, 17, 18, 19, 20, 21, 22, 23, 24, 26, 27, 28, 29, 30, 84, 87, 94, 101, 102, 106, 117
medical care, vii, 1, 3, 4, 8, 9, 11, 16, 19, 21, 28, 29, 85, 102
medical cost(s), vii, 1, 2, 3, 4, 5, 6, 7, 8, 9, 10, 11, 12, 13, 14, 15, 16, 17, 18, 19, 20, 21, 22, 23, 24, 26, 27, 28, 29, 103
Medical Expenditure Panel Survey (MEPS), viii, 2, 4, 5, 20, 21, 22, 23, 24, 25
medical expenditures, vii, 1, 4, 20, 21
Medicare, viii, 2, 4, 5, 15, 21, 24, 27, 30, 78, 84, 92, 117, 118, 119
medicine, 84, 93, 110, 113, 114, 117, 118
meta-analysis, 70, 71
metastasis, 14
methodology, 24, 26, 79
migrants, 96
military, 93, 109
military spending, 109
mission, 118
misuse, 89
model specification, 11
models, vii, 2, 3, 4, 5, 7, 8, 9, 12, 14, 15, 19, 25, 26, 27, 28, 30, 31, 95, 111, 114
modifications, 4
monopoly, 35
morbidity, 52, 107
mortality, 14, 15, 16, 17, 29, 50, 79
mortality rate, 16
motivation, 99, 100
musculoskeletal, 92

N

national income, 103
National Institutes of Health, 105
National Research Council (NRC), 102, 103
national security, 81
Netherlands, 29
neurodegenerative diseases, 105
New England, 29
next generation, 110
Nissen fundoplication, 51, 52
non-institutionalized, 20
normal distribution, 8, 10, 11
103
nurses, 95
nursing, 77, 84, 87, 95, 102
nursing care, 84
nursing home, 77

O

Obama, President Barack, 111
obesity, 52, 116
obstacles, 35, 97
OECD, 96
Office of Management and Budget, 30
operations, viii, 33, 49, 55
opportunities, 105, 109
outpatient, 10, 15, 21, 73
overweight, 116

P

pain, 35, 54, 55, 92

pain management, 94
pathology, 106
patient care, 82
pelvis, viii, 53
permit, 35
pharmaceutical, 84, 105
physical activity, 82
physical inactivity, 91
physicians, 54, 93, 107
pilot study, 70
placebo, 19, 20
PM, 71
poison, 115
policy, vii, 1, 3, 4, 5, 17, 18, 26, 28, 75, 79, 81, 82, 83, 84, 86, 88, 95, 97, 98, 100, 103, 106, 110, 117
policy makers, vii, 1, 3, 4, 17, 18, 26, 75
policymakers, 85
polio, 97
political system, 109
political uncertainty, 81
politics, 78, 111, 114, 117
population, 4, 6, 20, 26, 76, 82, 104
poverty, 76, 103
prayer, 88
pregnancy, 116
prescription drugs, 84
president, 30
president, 30, 111
prevention, 118
principles, 102, 114
private investment, 109
private sector, 92
probability, 4, 6, 8, 10, 18, 20, 24
probability distribution, 6
professionalization, 117
professionals, 72, 79, 93, 99, 102, 120
prolapse, 73
property taxes, 119
prostatectomy, 49, 70
protection, 84
public health, 35, 75, 82, 84
public investment, 110
public policy, 78, 88
public sector, 36, 56
P-value, 20, 23

Q

quality of life, vii, 2, 14, 17, 84, 105
quartile, 47, 48

R

race, 20, 22, 23, 68, 111
radiation, 28
radical hysterectomy, 71, 72
readership, 79
reality, 12, 35, 49, 55, 70, 109, 117
recall, 119
recession, 31, 54
recommendations, 82, 103, 109
recovery, 35, 55
rectal prolapse, 52
reform(s), 18, 84, 87, 95, 96, 97, 98, 107, 109, 110, 111, 112, 114, 117, 118
regression, 6, 8, 11, 21, 27, 28, 29, 31, 79
regression analysis, 29, 31
regression method, 6, 11
regression model, 6, 11, 79
regulations, 92
rehabilitation, 93
religion, 77, 115
renal cell carcinoma, 17
reputation, 92
research funding, 36, 69
researchers, viii, 2, 3, 11, 14, 18, 20, 25, 26, 91
resection, 42, 51
resource allocation, 3, 4, 17
resources, 21, 76, 93, 104, 109, 119
response, 4, 6, 22, 79
retirement, 76, 77, 78, 79, 119
revenue, 92, 109
rhetoric, 78, 87, 118
rights, 97
risk, vii, 2, 9, 14, 15, 16, 26, 27, 30, 79, 102, 116
risk factors, vii, 2, 9, 15, 26

RNA, 106
robotic assisted surgery, viii, 33, 34, 35, 49, 53, 54, 69
robotic assisted surgical technique, viii, 33
robotic surgery, viii, 33, 36, 49, 50, 51, 53, 54, 55, 56, 70, 71
robotics, viii, 33, 34, 36, 48, 49, 50, 53, 54, 69, 71
Romania, 97
rules, 75
Russia, 97

S

safety, 84, 107, 118
sample design, 20
SAS, 10
savings, 114
science, 29, 105, 113
scientific understanding, 106
scope, 85, 120
Secretary of Commerce, 110
security, 103
SEER-Medicare database, viii, 2, 5
self-control, 116
Senate, 80, 89, 98
services, 3, 8, 9, 16, 18, 24, 83, 91, 97, 99, 102, 103, 112
shadow economy, 98
shape, 9, 12, 86
shelter, 103
shortage, 78
showing, 78, 79
silver, 85
simulation, 7, 49, 70
Singapore, 96
skewness, 6, 26
Slovakia, 97
smoking, 91
smoothing, 12
social security, 76, 77, 78
society, 35, 54, 77, 115
socioeconomic status, 20
solution, 113
South Africa, 96
Soviet Union, 98
specialists, 93
specialization, 35, 55
spending, 4, 5, 18, 24, 29, 31, 81, 88, 102, 109
spirituality, 88
spleen, 52
Spring, 105
stability, 11
staffing, 87
standard deviation, 48
standard error, 48
state(s), 2, 76, 77, 92, 95, 98, 118
statistics, 76, 92
strategic management, 99, 100
stress, 98, 103, 116
stressors, 92
structure, 6, 7, 13, 27, 36, 54, 56, 76, 120
subgroups, 4, 20
Sun, 11, 12, 16, 17, 28, 31
surgical field, viii, 34, 36, 53, 54
surgical technique(s), viii, 33, 34, 49, 54, 56, 73
surplus, 71, 119
survey design, 79
survival, vii, 2, 14, 15, 16, 29
symptoms, 113
syndrome, 93

T

Taiwan, 96
target, 4
tax reform, 81
taxpayers, 119
team members, 36
techniques, 2, 35, 36, 51, 54, 56, 69, 72, 79, 94, 102
technological advancement, 69
technological advances, 2
technologies, 26, 34, 101
technology, viii, 17, 33, 34, 49, 53, 69, 79, 88, 99, 100, 108
tenure, 119
terrorism, 112

testing, vii, 2
therapeutics, 18, 105
therapy, 17, 19, 30, 89
threats, 78
total costs, 2
trade, 113
training, 34, 35, 36, 49, 54, 55, 69, 94
transformation, 6, 8, 10, 15, 27, 101, 115
transparency, 98
treatment, 3, 4, 11, 16, 17, 19, 20, 21, 24, 27, 49, 50, 51, 52, 55, 69, 70, 82, 84, 93, 96
tremor, viii, 34, 53, 54
trial, 13, 19, 50, 51, 52, 73
tuberculosis, 96
tuition, 78

U

uninsured, 24, 96
unions, 119
United Kingdom, 33, 53, 69
United Nations, 96
United States (USA), 5, 17, 28, 76, 78, 79, 80, 83, 84, 85, 86, 87, 88, 89, 91, 92, 96, 98, 100, 103, 105, 107, 108, 109, 111, 112, 114, 115, 117, 118

V

validation, 25
variables, 11, 12, 20
variations, 4, 35, 103
vector, 6, 8, 11, 12, 13, 20, 23
victims, 77
vote, 119
vulnerability, 102
vulnerable people, 110

W

wages, 79, 89
war, 115
Washington, 80, 81, 82, 85, 86, 88, 90, 98, 103, 104, 110, 117
waste, 101, 108, 118
web, 81, 90, 91, 113
weight gain, 116
weight loss, 52
well-being, 78, 110
wellness, 76, 90
White House, 30
WHO, 79
Wisconsin, 90, 118
workers, 80, 92
workforce, 101, 114
workplace, 90, 92
World Bank, 86
worldwide, 96

Y

Yale University, 112